You Only Know What You Know

MARCIA HUTCHISON

ISBN 978-1-68526-346-1 (Hardcover)
ISBN 978-1-68526-345-4 (Digital)

Cover painting "Disclosure" is an original work of the author.

Covenant Books
11661 Hwy 707
Murrells Inlet, SC 29576
www.covenantbooks.com

To my grandsons—Jason Collins, Justin
and Joel Babin, and Lawson Eddy
To my great-grandsons, Coyt John Hamlin,
Noah Eddy, Trey Thomas, Lawson Wade,
and Jaydon and Austin Aydellott
To my great-great-grandsons, Miles, Maddox, and Ever.
We will not believe more than we know.
We will not live higher than our beliefs.

CONTENTS

DEAR GRANDSONS

We may be miles apart, but love knows no boundaries. You are of my blood. Without me, there would be no you. Without our ancestors, there would be no us. Have you ever given this any thought or been curious about our ancestors, who came from foreign lands to build a new world, a new life? All humankind possesses an innate force that pushes him forward in pursuit of his aspirations. Sometimes our inclinations are for the good, and sometimes they lead to the dark side of life. The choices we make today will affect the outcomes of all our tomorrows.

Please know that these words are written with love and not in any way meant to be disparaging. My purpose is to hopefully challenge your mind, inspire your intellect to search beyond what you can see, feel, taste, and hear, looking beyond the moment. Search out our family history and their qualities, love of God, veracity, fortitude, and sense of dignity. Explore world and ancient world history. I promise you will be enlightened on many things. Make today about the rest of your life.

CHAPTER 1

Nothing New Under The Sun

That which has been is what will be,
That which is done is what will be done,
And there is nothing new under the sun.
—Ecclesiastes 1:9

All victories and defeats, past and present, have taken long, costly, and painful journeys, and who will remember their demise? All hostile aggressors have different faces with the same mindset: total control. The paradigms have never changed throughout the history of humankind. Man revels in his victories, then comes the insurrection.

Study the American Indian, who arrived on this continent thousands of years ago from Asia via Beringia (a land bridge connecting Asia to North America). According to scientific discoveries, the ancestral roots of all Native Americans descended from a single gene pool. Can you imagine? The idea of a single gene pool today would be inconceivable. Most young people never give a thought to their cultural history. The ancestral history of these amazingly brave people exhibit mankind's innate desire for a better life and, above all, a free existence.

Unfortunately, total freedoms as the Indian once knew are gone, their pride and beliefs as a society, threatened. The white man, in pursuit of his own resolve, hunted down, slaughtered, and forced the Indians off their lands onto designated areas managed by a federally recognized Indian tribe under the US Bureau of Indian Affairs, including Alaska Native villages.

Study the plight of the American Indian and understand the evils that can and will befall any country and its people at any time, including today! Once the Indians were confined, disease and malnutrition were the biggest culprits that wiped out an estimated 90 percent of the Native Americans, not warfare. These people had never before been exposed to the old-world pathogens spread by the settlers and their cows, pigs, sheep, goats, and horses. Millions of Native Americans died from measles, influenza, whooping cough, diphtheria, typhus, bubonic plague, cholera, and scarlet fever. Diseases like smallpox were deliberately spread through blankets to extirpate this execrable race of people. The detestable white man was the culprit and not the Indians, who lived on lands they discovered and cultivated according to their customs.

The French and Indian war was the North American conflict in a larger imperial war between Great Britain and France known as the Seven Years' War. It ended with the treaty of Paris. In the aftermath of the French and Indian

War (1754–1763), no European had yet settled in the frontier of Pennsylvania. A new wave of Scots and Irish immigrants encroached on Native American land in the backcountry, often in blatant violation of previously signed treaties. These settlers claimed that Indians often raided their homes, killing men, women, and children. What did the settlers expect? The Indians had an innate right to protect their land, land brutally stolen from them.

John Elder, who was the parson at Paxtang, became the leader of a band of killers. He was known as the "Fighting Parson" and kept his rifle in the pulpit. Trust me, Jesus was certainly not blessing that bunch of sinners. Although there had been no Indian attacks in the area, the Paxton Boys claimed that the Conestoga secretly provided aid and intelligence to other Native Americans who had been pillaging and scalping.

"On December 14, 1763, about fifty-seven blind drunk vigilantes slaughtered twenty innocent and defenseless Conestoga Indians. Groups of raging drunks attacked the Conestogas homes, murdering, scalping, mutilating, and burning cabins. Many of these slaughtered Indians had become Christians living peacefully with their white neighbors. The Conestoga lived on land ceded by William Penn to their ancestors in the 1690s" (Editors of Encyclopedia Britannica). This horrible Pennsylvania atrocity remains a blot on American soil we can never erase.

Woe to Pastor Elder, playing God with his rifle under the pulpit. No way was he walking with the Lord. Elder was a self-righteous bigot. Like the Paxton Boys, our world is filled with the same angry bigots screaming for power and justice—*their* justice, not God's.

What separates these people from the dreaded KKK? Absolutely nothing! Our Creator God makes His sun rise on the evil and on the good. "He sends rain on the just and the unjust alike" (Matthew 5:45). Who in this power-hungry political world believes anything the Bible has to say? A closed mind will never know.

The Trail of Tears

This heartbreaking story perfectly depicts man's inhumanity to man. Between 1830 and 1850, the United States government forced one hundred thousand tribes off their homelands to Indian territories in Oklahoma. When the white men wanted land, they just took it. The Choctaw, Chickasaw, and Creeks were forced to march in chains 5,043 miles, covering nine states to the western plains. They had little or no food. Who cared! Disease and starvation were rampant; thousands died along the way. In 1851, Congress passed the Indian Appropriations Act and provided funds to move Indians tribes onto farming reservations and hopefully keep them under control. There were true believers among the settlers who brought the Indians to salvation through Christ and took no part in this horrendous plan.

It is amazing how anyone could embrace anything the evil white man had to say. The so-called Christian white man talked out both sides of his mouth. This gruesome display of evil is a direct result of hatred, narrow-mindedness, division, and self-absorbed ignorance. Our children are inundated today in our schools with this same kind of garbage. The young children of my day were completely immersed in the Indian-cowboy movies. Kill the Indians! We cheered when the Indians were slaughtered by the so-called good guys. Cowboys were portrayed as heroes. Not for years did I fully understand the ability to wield force through brainwashing tactics. It never crossed my mind. Don't for one second ignore this enormity. "You only know what you know. What has been will be again."

We have seen the result of the pastor with his gun under the pulpit. Compare modern-day controlling elites with the white man's ruthless takeover of Indian land.

Bill Gates is the biggest private owner of farmland in the United States, a 2018 purchase of 14,599 acres of prime Eastern Washington farmland for $171 million—traditional Yakama territory. In total, Bill Gates owns approximately 242,000 acres of farmland with assets totaling more than $690 million. To put that into perspective, that's nearly the size of Hong Kong and twice the acreage of the Lower Brule Sioux Tribe. A white man owns more farmland that the entire native American Nation. Bill Gates has never been a farmer. *The Land Report* dubbed him "Farmer Bill" this year. The third richest man on the planet doesn't have a green thumb, nor does he put in the backbreaking labor humble people, who gets far less praise for it, do to grow our food. That kind of work isn't what made Bill Gates rich.

The United States is defined by the excesses of its ruling class. Let me make it perfectly clear that I am not defined in any way by this class of people nor their beliefs. I own my home on a small zero-lot-line, and I am grateful for it.

Why do a handful of people own so much land? Land is power, land is wealth, and greed propels men to climb higher and higher. The American dream is the belief that anyone, regardless of where they were born or what class they were born into, can attain their own version of success, and we can. Freedom includes the rights, liberty, and the opportunity for prosperity and success achieved through dedication and hard work as long as our country is free. Never envy the rich man's success. Learn contentment, and you will be fulfilled. Our freedoms are in jeopardy today like no other time in the history of our nation.

At one time, the relationship to land—who owns it, who works it, and who cares for it—reflected the American dream. Although my grandfather wasn't a rich man, he was a profitable landowner. He was well respected by all races as an industrious, innovative man, honest almost to a fault. As a God-fearing man, he believed in the equality of all men and treated all men with dignity. This is not to say inequality doesn't exist now or in Grandfather's day.

The legacies of colonialism, white supremacy in the United States, the world at large cannot be denied. Wealth accumulation often goes hand in hand with exploitation and dispossession. In this country, enslaved black labor first built US wealth atop stolen native land. Yet there are former slaves who acquired land, prospered, and their offspring pursued higher education and now teach in our universities. These hardworking American citizens are not running around, screaming reparations. They are too busy forging ahead!

The 1862 Homestead Acts opened up 270 million acres of indigenous territory, which amounts to 19 percent of US land, for white settlement. Black people, Mexicans, Asian, and Native people were categorically excluded from the benefits of federal programs that subsidized and protected generations of white wealth. As far as I'm concerned, this is yet another blot on humanity. The colonists came from foreign territorial lands belonging to the monarchs. Apparently, considering it was now their right to entitlements, they embraced the only example they knew. You only know what you know.

Ted Turner

"The billionaire media mogul Ted Turner epitomizes such disparities. He owns two million acres and has the world's largest privately owned buffalo herd. These animals, which are sacred to my people and were nearly hunted to extinction by settlers, are preserved today on two hundred thousand acres of Turner ranchland within the boundaries of the 1868 Fort Laramie Treaty territory in the western half of what is now the state of South Dakota, land that was once guaranteed by the US Government to be a 'permanent home' for Lakota people" (Opinion by Nick Estes).

The gun and the whip may not accompany land acquisitions this time around, but billionaire-class assertions that philosopher kings and climate-conscious investors think they know better than the original caretakers—little more than a ruse. This amounts to a twenty-first-century land grab, with big payouts in a for-profit economy seeking *green* solutions.

This present era is dominated by the ultrarich, the climate crisis (a red herring uncontrollable by man), and a burgeoning green capitalism. And Bill Gates's new book *How to Avoid a Climate Disaster* positions him as a thought leader in how to stop putting greenhouse gases into the atmosphere. He claims to know how to fund what he has called elsewhere a "global green revolution" to help poor farmers mitigate climate change. There is no climate change, but wealthy fools will ride the concept until the bitter end, lining their pockets along the way. What expertise in climate change, science, or agriculture does Bill Gates possess beyond being filthy rich? Its beyond anyone's guess.

When pressed during a book discussion on Reddit about why he's gobbling up so much farmland, Gates claimed, "It's not connected to climate" (change). The decision, he said, came from his "investment group." Cascade Investment, the firm making these acquisitions, is *controlled* by Gates. And the firm said it's "very supportive of sustainable farming." He is also a shareholder in the plant-based protein companies Beyond Meat and Impossible Foods as well as the farming equipment manufacturer John Deere. Gates largest farmland acquisition happened in 2017, when it acquired sixty-one farming properties from a Canadian investment firm to the tune of $500 million.

Arable land is not just profitable; there's a more cynical calculation. Investment firms are making the argument farmlands will meet "carbon-neutral" targets for sustainable investments portfolios while anticipating an increase of agricultural productivity and revenue. And while Bill Gates frets about eating hamburgers in his book for the amount of greenhouse gases the meat industry produces, largely for the consumption of rich countries, his massive carbon footprint has little to do with his personal diet and is not forgivable by simply buying more land to sequester more carbon. I read an article stating Bill Gates also owns massive shares in the COVID vaccines. Why not? His hand is everywhere. There is more written on the Indian subject, but enough said; you get the message.

The world's richest 1 percent emit double the carbon of the poorest 50 percent. According to *Forbes*, the world's billionaires saw their wealth swell by $1.9 trillion in 2020, while more than twenty-two million US workers (mostly women) lost their jobs. Did you vote for a democrat? Shame on you.

Small farmers and indigenous caretakers are more cautious with the use of land. For indigenous caretakers, land use isn't premised on a return of investments; it's about maintaining the land for the next generation, meeting the needs of the present, and a respect for the diversity of life. What a beautiful concept. Too bad our power-hungry leaders refuse to see it this way.

The average person has nothing in common with megalandowners like Bill Gates or Ted Turner. Massive land ownership should not be the sole property of a few.

The extensive tax avoidance by these titans of industry will always far exceed their supposed charitable donations to the public. The "'billionaire knows best" mentality personifies the deep-seated realities of colonialism and white supremacy, and it ignores those who actually know best how to use and live with the land. These billionaires have nothing to offer us in terms of saving the planet, unless it's giving our land back.

America has always been a hodgepodge of ethnicities, mostly Europeans, who came to the New World for a fresh start away from dictatorial monarchs. While this is common among humanity, what was done to the American Indians was horrendous as was the black slave trade. They were treated as nonhumans. Indians were not allowed to leave the reservation without permission. Despite this injustice, there were decent, God-fearing people who refused to endorse these ugly, biased movements. Condoning and promoting the evils of division will never bring harmony to any peoples. Promoting division is front and center today.

Don't be naive enough to think that political differences in our country will not succumb to this same insanity. I witnessed a self-absorbed female Democrat stupid enough to say on TV that Republicans need to be interned and reprogramed. This prevailing mentality will be the demise of the Democratic Party next election. Americans are neither brainless nor blind.

"Divide and conquer," (Julius Caesar). Reprograming is exactly what happened to past civilizations over and over again. The evil side of human nature remains the same. Those who refused to comply were simply slaughtered, not reprogramed. We interned the Japanese during WWII, rightly so for their inhumane treatment of war prisoners. Today, America's freedom of speech is thrown out the window by the controlling elite. What's next? No one will knock at your door; evil powers will simply barge right in unannounced, confiscate your property, or move a family of refuges in to share your property. This is exactly what the communists in Russia did, Hitler did, and what we did to the American Indian. Check out the 1965 movie *Doctor Zhivago*. It's all there.

Before the casinos, American Indians lived in abject squalor. During the 1940s, our family traveled west on several summer vacations. We traveled through reservations, where I witnessed the degradation firsthand. They lived in a motley collection of beat-up old trailer homes, melting snow for bathwater when wells froze over because they lacked indoor plumbing. Three quarters of tribal members received government food supplements. Wonder what happened to the other quarter? With nothing constructive to do, Indians became alcoholics from the white man's liquor—in later years, drug addicts and drug dealers. This is the eventual downfall of all cultures once they become dependent upon the welfare state, the government. Only the controlling elite reap the rewards, a perfect picture of oligarch rule or socialism, the final step before communism.

Although the American Indian's quality of life has greatly improved, many still live on reservations. Under the BIA, tribes are sovereign and not subject to federal laws. From degradation to billions, an American success story— or is it? Money is only a temporary fix. Indian gaming was legalized in 1988, after which a few bingo halls and small casinos were scattered across Indian country. In thirty-one years, twenty-eight states have a total of 460 tribal casinos, generating revenues of more than 430 billion. Commercial casinos owned by corporations or individuals; tribal casinos owned by Indian tribes. The Indian defeated poverty through their own initiative and creativity. Will they now be able to defeat the pitfalls of wealth? Where will they stand when the one-world government takes over and perhaps confiscates their wealth?

The purpose in writing only a portion of these truths is to provoke a critical awareness of world history, of cultures, and draw parallels with today. The powerful promote their agendas with massive amounts of money, conflict, blatant lies, half-truths, brainwashing, even brutal executions. Clearly, all societies, from ancient times until today, have or will encounter threats by a type of systematic evil aggression. This has been mankind's arduous search for fame, fortune, and control throughout the history of the world. Triumph at all costs. Big words! Once evil gains total power, it will roll over humanity like a giant tidal wave, just like they did the Indian. Total control always has and always will.

The little man, the worker, no matter his ethnicity, is of no consequence. Conquer, defeat; conquer, conquer, defeat. The average person will never, ever come out on top. As soon as a society is thoroughly brainwashed, lied to, no longer necessary, defeated, ambitions smashed, the establishment takes total control, and injustice hangs heavy in the air. A wise person will prioritize his life now rather than later.

> The eye never has enough of seeing
> Nor the ear its fill of hearing,
> What has been will be again,
> What has been done will be done again,
> There is nothing new under the sun.
> (Ecclesiastes 1:8–9)

CHAPTER 2

A World under Siege

Bioterrorism is nothing new. Germ warfare is nothing new. America is also guilty of other atrocities and will one day answer to God. It is probable this COVID virus was deliberately unleashed on the entire world, opening the floodgates of mass hysteria, priming the people to accept a controlling government. Destroying our cities, businesses, and schools is a prerequisite to the evil campaign now in progress.

And that is *control?* The COVID pandemic has aided evil to repeat itself. As evidence has proven, China and other evil entities are responsible for releasing COVID upon the world. This virus was engineered in a lab at Wuhan, China. The news reports that Dr. Fauci gave the Chinese $6 million for research on this virus. Hopefully, his time is limited.

I just learned of another "Dr. Fauci horror story." The animal research regulator says the Fauci Institute funded "deadly and unnecessary" experiments on dogs. Advocacy group White Coat Waste cited government documents that the institute led by President Joe Biden's chief medical adviser, Dr. Anthony Fauci, funded a study in which dozens of dogs were unnecessarily tortured.

Dr. Anthony Fauci operated the National Institute of Allergy and Infectious Disease since 1984. He personally gave the NIAID $424,455. Under the Freedom of Information Act (FOIA), the WCW obtained documents on animal testing.

E-mails obtained by WCW indicate that the study started in November 2020 and is scheduled to end in early 2022. According to the documents, approximately twenty-eight beagles will be infected and euthanized after 196 days for blood collection and analysis. This means that these dogs were killed in June of 2021. The dogs suffered unbearable pain for 196 days. The name of the vaccine has been edited. However, according to the daily caller, the vaccine is called Fugard.

Fauci has become a polarizing figure in the United States. The Democrats praised him as a heroic scientist who would never make mistakes on COVID-19 or any other issues. At the same time, the Republicans accused him of ambivalent stances in the fight against the coronavirus and funding what they called the acquisition of functionality (gain of function) research of the Wuhan Institute. Guilty?

However, if a scientist gets his wish, criticism of Fauci may soon become a federal hate crime. This is the point of the proposal published in *PLOS Biology* by Dr. Peter Hotez, professor of pediatrics and molecular virology at Baylor College of Medicine. Holocaust survivor and activist Eli Wiesel said, "Neutrality or silence is good for the oppressor." I find this a ray of light in all this darkness. Wake up, Americans. Proverbs 23:12 apply your heart to instruction, and your ears to words of knowledge.

A world under siege will either come out fighting or cower under the opposition. Peace is my banner! Innocent people in this country will face new tricks by nefarious forces at any time and any place. Defeating the COVID crisis will not alter plans for destroying America. It is certainly feasible the virus may be part of the plan to bring down America. You can control some of the people some of the time but never all of the people all the time. As you will see, powerful men in pursuit of total control will never look back at the death and destruction left in their wake. The New World Order being systemically crammed down our throats is only the beginning. The Bible addresses the New World Order. There is nothing new under the sun.

If do-overs were possible, I choose from birth through eight. The first eight years of my life were a kinder and gentler time to live and grow up in. Our story, like many others, is a portrait of early-twentieth-century America as we lived it. If we live long enough, what we see today will disappear tomorrow into the recycling bins of the future. The quest to validate truths through ancient history became my obsession.

Obsessive people in search of a better life will move heaven and earth to achieve their goal. As we travel the roads of antiquity, think of our journey as a passport through bygone days and through all the tomorrows yet to come. For now, let's journey with the Hutchison's from Scotland to America.

CHAPTER 3

The Hutchisons

When did the Hutchisons migrate to this continent? I was able to trace our journey back only so far. We have always been proud of our Scottish heritage. For now, I have little information of Hutchison life in Scotland. We will live vicariously through recorded history of ancient times in Scotland. I do believe our ancestors were farmers in Southern Scotland.

Since there is a book available on mother's family, "The Lotts and the Lards" (not a published book), I will concentrate mostly on our father's side. We came from a resilient people made of good Scottish stock, and have come to embrace our ancestral history. We might discover where our characteristics came from, both the noble and the ignoble, and certainly Scottish grit. No one is perfect, and neither were our families—far from it. All of humanity are flawed human beings, and that includes all the Hutchisons. No matter how far back we push all our yesterdays, ugly memories will repeatedly show its face until we make a concerted effort to rid ourselves of all garbage forever; remember, only garbage, not people. We can choose to live baggage free or stifle our mental growth with not only yesterday's poisons but todays disinformation as well. Placing blame only serves to fan the fires of ignorance. Clean house! Believe me, it is very liberating. Never, ever forget, "no man is an island" (John Donne, English poet, seventeenth century, four-hundred-year-old poem against isolation).

The surname Hutchison is of English and Scottish origin. The name derives from the medieval given name Huchin, a diminutive of Hugh first found in Glasgow, where James Huchonsone held land in 1454. John Huchonsone was burgess of Aberdeen in 1466. George Huchunson was burgess of Glasgow in 1477, then he reappeared as George Hutcheson the following year. The purpose of this list, which goes on and on, was to point out the spelling variations. Records from the Gaelic era show an enormous number of spelling variations, even in names referring to the same person. Hutchison is an Anglo-Scottish surname. It is a patronymic and diminutive form of the original personal name Hugh. Hugh is Norman French but of pre-seventh-century Old German origin. Hutche, a variant of Hugh. *Patronymic* (pa-truh-ni-muhk) means derived from a father's or ancestor's name.

Before we learn about the Hutchison history and our migration, we need to learn facts. Our ancestors originally came from Southern Scotland. Both Ireland and Scotland belonged to English royalty. These very complicated relationships were consistently manipulated for one reason or another, mostly to benefit the crown. This changed the course of our family's history. England owned and ruled Ireland, Scotland, and Wales. We are blessed to be Americans now, so no complaints.

British Rule

Royal children were pawns on the world stage. Having no choice, they learned early the benefits of power, greed, and wealth. "The apple doesn't fall far from the tree." Beware, parents: this still holds true today.

Mary, Queen of Scots, also known as Mary Stuart or Mary I of Scotland. She was the only surviving legitimate child of King James V of Scotland and Mary of Guise of France. Her reign: 1542–1567. Henry VIII was her great uncle. Elizabeth I was her cousin. She was six days old when her father died, and she ascended to the throne, becoming the infant queen of Scotland in 1542.

Mary I, Queen of England, House of Tudor, was the daughter of Catherine of Aragon and Henry VIII of England. She was the first ever queen of England to rule in her own right. Mary has long been known only as "Bloody Mary." She persecuted Protestant heretics, whom she burned at the stake by the hundreds, mostly common citizens. Her own father executed eighty-one people for heresy. Mary was a Catholic monarch succeeded by a Protestant queen in a country that remained Protestant.

Elizabeth I also executed scores of people for their faith, including her cousin Queen Mary I. Mary had sought the protection of England's Queen Elizabeth I, who instead had her arrested and thrown in prison. Elizabeth, in her self-centered paranoia, feared losing what she had or not being able to get what she wanted and imprisoned her cousin. Evil intentions will maintain control at all costs, no matter who or what you may be. Mary spent the rest of her life in captivity until her 1558 execution.

All over Europe, punishment for heresy was not only death but of the destruction of the corpse to prevent the use of their body parts for relics. Really, how barbaric is that gruesome thought? No wonder societies have consistently contributed to their own demise. The people and royalty alike obviously lacked knowledge of God's Word in this so-called Christian nation.

The British aristocracy is the highest class in British society, especially those holding hereditary titles or office. A country with this form of government is an oligarchy or plutocracy, ruled by the few or the wealthy. A government ruled by a privileged minority of upper class, usually of inherited social position, this is a group of people who believe they are above others. Oligarchy may very well be the future of America once our freedoms are crushed. We have several billionaires ready to take over once the destruction of our country is complete—of course, all believing their money sets them above the common people: us! See Glen Beck on Black Rock "world order"—a ponzi scheme.

English royalty owned and controlled Scotland, Ireland, and Wales. These were very complicated relationships that were consistently manipulated for one reason or another to benefit powerful people. Royal children were pawns on the royal stage, as were the Scots and the Irish. Mary Stewart was the only surviving child of King James V of Scotland and his second wife Mary of Guise. James Charles Stuart was king of three countries—King of Scotland as James VI and King of England and Ireland as James from the union of Scottish and English crowns until his death.

Mary's claims to the English throne were as strong as her claims to the Scottish throne. As Henry VII of England's great-granddaughter, Mary was next in line to the English throne, after Henry VIII's children. The Scottish nobility decided that they must make peace with England and agreed that Mary should marry Henry VIII's son, her cousin, and the future Edward VI.

No sooner had the treaty been arranged, the Catholics opposed the plan. They took Mary, a Catholic, to Stirling Castle. To Henry's fury, they broke the match, preferring to return to Scotland's traditional alliance with France.

Henry, in his fury, ordered the savage series of attacks into Scotland known as the Rough Wooing. He set fire to the abbey where James V was buried, burned crops, and set ablaze the border abbeys of Melrose, Jedburgh, and Dryburgh.

Undeterred, the Scots in 1548 betrothed Mary to the French King Henry II (heir, the Dauphine Francis) and sent her to be brought up at the French court. It is said the spelling of the family name of Stewart changed to Stuart at that time to suit French conventional spelling. There was no W in the French language.

Mary married the Dauphin in Paris, May 24, 1558. Mary was now queen of both France and Scotland, but her reign was brief, for the Dauphin died of an ear infection in 1560. Despite the warnings, Catholic Mary decided to return to Scotland, now officially a Protestant country.

I think there is a good series on the life of Mary and the Dauphin of France. Seems like the Dauphin's mother was involved in all the castle intrigue. I did enjoy it.

At first, Mary ruled Scotland successfully and with moderation, advised by her half brother Lord James. Then she married her second cousin Henry Stewart, Lord of Darnley. Henry Stuart (Stewart, grandson of Henry VII) initiated a tragic series of events made worse by factious Scotland nobles. Lord Darnley became the tool of Mary's enemies. They burst into her supper chambers, threatened the pregnant Mary, and murdered her secretary. After the birth of their son James, their troubled relationship did not change. When Darnley was murdered, the people suspected that Mary was implicated in the crime.

Three months later Mary married the Earl of Bothwell, generally believed to be Darnley's principal murderer. This brought about her inevitable ruin. Her Protestant lords rose up against her. In 1557, she surrendered, was imprisoned, and was forced to abdicate in favor of her infant son. Bothwell fled to Scandinavia, where he was arrested and held prisoner until his death.

Mary escaped from prison in 1568, only to be defeated in another battle. She then sought shelter in England, believing Queen Elizabeth (her cousin) would support her cause, but instead, she was kept in captivity for nineteen years. Mary was finally executed in 1587 at the age of forty-four. This Mary, Queen of Scots was not "Bloody Mary."

James was the son of Mary Queen of Scots and a great great grandson of Henry VII. Henry was King of England and Lord of Ireland, and thus a potential successor to all three thrones. James succeeded to the Scottish throne at the age of thirteen months, after his mother was compelled to abdicate in his favor.

From birth, Mary was never free to be her own person. The powerful manipulated her life from age six until her death. How cruel! Of course, these children grow into tyrannical adults because they certainly had the example set before them—it's all they know. Personally, I do not believe either of their religious arguments hold water, Protestant or Catholic. The crown, the government, or the populists go around murdering people to serve their own purpose. This is not serving the Christ I know. All children learn by example. This segment of British history paints past and present pictures of evil, godless people, lacking any semblance of morals. Powerful men will execute control at all costs. It is a miracle royal families were not plagued with idiots because of the incestuous marriages. As you will learn, "there is nothing new under the son."

Bloody Mary

Mary I, queen of England, Tudor, was known as Bloody Mary. She was Henry VIII's daughter with his first wife, Catherine of Aragon. Mary took the throne in 1553, reigning as the first queen regent of England and Ireland.

Seeking to return England to the Catholic Church, she persecuted hundreds of Protestants.

A young Henry was forced to marry Catherine, who was the widow of his deceased brother. Royal children had no rights. Mary, as a child, was a pawn in England's bitter rivalry with more powerful nations. She was fruitlessly proposed in marriage to this or that potentate desired as an ally. Mary was a bright girl, educated by her mother, and a governess of ducal rank. Mary finally married the Holy Roman emperor, her cousin Charles the VI (Charles I of Spain). He promptly commanded her to come with a huge cash dowry. This demand was ignored; he then jilted her and found a more advantageous match. Isn't all this just too bizarre? This so-called Holy Roman emperor was definitely not holy and in no way a true Christian. Money and power were his god, as it was for many in those days.

In 1525, Mary was named Princess of Wales by her father. The lack of documents suggests she was never formally invested. She then held court at Ludlow Castle. Yes, believe it, new betrothal plans were made. Mary's life was constantly radically disrupted. Now she had to contend with her father's marriage to Anne Boleyn and Henry's divorcing her mother. The illegal allegation of incest made Mary illegitimate. This was a lie; there was no incest. The purpose was for Henry to marry Anne Boleyn. Henry simply changed the law.

This was absurd as all the royals consist of incestuous marriages. This was an example of an old saying: "the pot calls the kettle black." Meanwhile, Anne Boleyn, the new queen, forbade Mary access to her and to her parents, stripped her of her title of princess, and forced her to function as a lady-in-waiting to the infant Elizabeth, Henry's new daughter.

Mary never saw her mother again. Despite great danger, they secretly corresponded. Anne's hatred pursued Mary so relentlessly that Mary feared execution. Mary never admitted to illegitimacy, nor would she enter a convent when ordered to do so. Finally in control, anger and resentment ruled her life. Is it not a wonder she became a brutal ruler? Mary was no more brutal than other cruel monarchs who placed no value on human life.

Henry, no longer a Catholic monarch, was the onset of the Protestant church of England and I suppose all Protestants thereafter. Protestant: protesting Catholicism. In Tudor England, bloody punishments were the norm, with execution methods ranging from beheading to boiling and to hanging. It's estimated that Tudor England executed as many as seventy-two thousand subjects. There were many more executions by other monarchs. Questioning a monarch's established religious policies was tantamount to rejecting the divinity-ordained authority. Down south, we call this *hogwash*.

This was truly a brutal age, and more of the same could be coming our way if we do not put a stop to the present regime's plans to destroy our nation. Mary I of England has long been known only as "Bloody Mary." She persecuted Protestant heretics, whom she burned at the stake by the hundreds, mostly common citizens or they died in prison. Her own father executed seventy-two thousand people for heresy. Elizabeth I also executed scores of people for their faith, including her cousin Queen Mary I.

Elizabeth I of England and Mary, Queen of Scots, were two of the greatest, most legendary rivals in recorded history, although they never even met. Their tortured relationship was determined long before, during childhood, which formed both queen's characters and seal Mary's tragic fate.

We are not supposed to act upon our feelings but legitimize what we believe to be true and righteous. You only know what you know. Mary sought protection from her cousin Elizabeth. Elizabeth, in her self-centered paranoia, feared losing what she had or feared not being able to get what she wanted and threw Mary in prison. In this world, one maintains control at all costs. Mary spent the rest of her life, nineteen years, in captivity until her 1587 execution. Mary was beheaded.

As unmarried monarchs, they faced the same pressure to marry, not only to produce an heir but to give their reign masculine authority. You could say Mary burned Protestants, and Elizabeth disemboweled Catholics. Isn't this bloody picture lovely? These women were not God-centered people but were totally self-centered, ruled by evil forces. God-centered compassion was nonexistent. You only know what you know. The masses lacking resolution and/or education will inevitably follow the next despot who promises them peace and affluence.

True to form, the next generation either forgets or ignores that "total power corrupts" until it's too late. It is doubtful Mary and Elizabeth ever experienced a truly peaceful existence. They were never taught nor witnessed the grace of godly contentment. Thirst for power and greed will destroy families and mighty nations alike. Praise God I have lived these eighty-seven years in relative peace despite my shortcomings and detours hindering my journey along the way. Mistakes are inevitable because we are fallen humans living in a fallen world, free to make mistakes, free to choose.

The British aristocracy is the highest class in British society, especially those holding hereditary titles or office. Power and money still speak loud and clear today. A country with this form of government is an oligarchy or plutocracy, ruled by the few or the wealthy, a government ruled by a privileged minority of upper class, usually of inherited and social position. This is a group of people who make a big noise and believe they are above others, as do extremely wealthy people, and some silly Hollywood ditto people. Oligarchy may very well be the future of America once our freedoms are crushed and our Constitution shredded for the benefit of billionaires working overtime to take over our country once the destruction is complete. This mindset will destroy our nation, and this is what we face today. "There is nothing new under the sun."

Hutchison Migration

All this was to say Scotland, Wales, and Ireland were ruled by England. King James VI ruled Scotland. In 1603, he became King James of England, beginning a new dynasty: the Stuarts. King James was responsible for a new translation of the Bible. The King James Version was published in 1605.

At least a dozen Hutchisons are from the 1680s period, when David and James Hutchison fled Scotland for Northern Ireland. I cannot put them into our family tree, but it's possible that they are our ancestors. Our family, controlled by the English throne, was in the first major influx of border English and Lowland Scots into Ulster. They were mostly Presbyterians. Before the Plantations of Ulster and even before the Flight of the Earls, there was the 1606 independent Scottish settlements in East Down and Antrim. Led by adventurers James Hamilton and Sir Hugh Montgomery, two Ayrshire lairds, the migration started around 1605.

After leaving Scotland, the Hutchisons settled in Antrim County, Ireland; date is uncertain. How long a time in Antrim County is uncertain. We do have family buried there. The Scots migrated to Ireland in large numbers because of the government-sanctioned plantations of Ulster, a planned process of colonization that took place under the auspices of James VI of Scotland, James I of England (same man), on land confiscated from members of the Gaelic nobility of Ireland. An estimated half a million acres were confiscated from the Gaelic nobility, most of whom had fled Ireland in 1607. Another example of powerful men confiscating land, destroying a culture, and once again changing history.

Does this not sound familiar? British expanse around the globe meant that the sun was always shinning on one of its territories. As a free American Christian, I would certainly resent any secular intrusion upon my life. Controlling forces are snapping at the heels of our freedoms today.

The Scots and Irish chose to join the migration to North America from Ireland, some on the frontiers where they could protect the more settled areas from the American Indian and on land we stole from the Indians. Our family first settled in South Carolina, then to Choctaw County, Northern Mississippi.

The Hutchisons had no contact with the American Indians. As the name Choctaw implies, Indians occupied this territory at one time. When Europeans began settling America in the sixteenth century, the Choctaw were living in the Southeastern United States, largely in areas that became Mississippi. The Choctaw were farmers and hunters. In the eighteenth-century wars between the French and the British, the Choctaws allied themselves with the French. Following the defeat of the French (1754–63), the Choctaw land was taken from them by the British, forcing some to move westward in search of new land.

In the 1801 Treaty of Fort Adams, the Choctaws ceded to the United States 2,641,920 acres of land. There were also other lands ceded to the government. The Treaty of Dancing Rabbit Creek in 1830 marked the final cession of lands and outlined the terms of Choctaw removal to the west. The Choctaw Nation was the first Indian tribe removed by the federal government from its ancestral home to land set aside for them in what is now Oklahoma. The Hutchison's owned a thousand plus acres in Choctaw territory

A Bit of Scottish History

The root of the ancient Dalradian-Scottish name Hutchison is a variation of a name first used by Vikings settlers in ancient Scotland, all derived from a diminutive form of Hugh or from the Old French word *Huchon*. Hutchinson would, of course, mean "son of Hugh." The suffix *son* indicates "son of." Hutchinson was first found in Northumberland.

Dalradian in geology describes a series of metamorphic rocks typically developed in the high ground southeast of the Great Glen of Scotland. The Great Glen follows eighty miles of lochs and rivers. It's a fantastic natural route through the Scottish Highlands, with exceptional scenery and gorgeous forests.

Who were the Gales? For centuries, historians have debated the Gales' origin. The Gales came from Ireland around AD 500 under King Fergus Mór and conquered Argyll from the Picts. They called themselves Goidi, then Gales, and later called Scotland Alba. Recently, archaeologists have challenged this idea.

The Gales gave Scotland its name from *Scots*, a racially derogatory term used by the Romans in the third and fourth centuries. Scotland (Caledonia) was inhabited for thousands of years before the Romans arrived. Scotland was first recorded in writing during the Greco-Roman period, eighth century BC to the sixth century AD. The area of Britain now known as Scotland was called Caledonia (Latin). During Roman occupation of Scotland, the area called Caledonia was physically separated from the rest of the island by the Antonine

Wall. The people were known as the Caledonians. ("Old Caledonia," a folk song written in 1977 by Dougie MacLean.)

After three decades of war, the Romans, in AD 71, conquered the tribes of Britain, England, and Wales. Rome invaded Caledonia, falsely claiming victory. It is now believed the Romans at no point controlled even half of present-day Scotland. The Scots were controlled by thirty thousand fierce warrior tribes, who refused to bow to the Roman Empire. In AD 211, the Roman army finally packed up and left. The Romans may have established the greatest empire the ancient world had ever seen, but they never really managed to conquer Scotland. The result was that Scotland managed to hold on to its independence, a feat which instilled a national pride that remains to this day. I also proudly lay claim to our good old Scottish grit.

The name *Picts* means painted ones in Latin because the tribes were known for painting their entire bodies with tattoos. The Picts were in fact the indigenous population who arrived in Britain before the Romans. Indigenous to northern Scotland, they originally came from Scythia (Scandinavia). Since they left no written record of their history, what is known comes from later Roman and Scottish writers and from stone carvings.

Picts were first mentioned in 297 BC until they supposedly vanished during the tenth century. The Picts did not mysteriously disappear; they merged with the southern Scots culture, who already had a written history. The Picts held their territory against the Romans in a number of battles. They were once defeated in battle yet won the war. Scotland holds the distinction of never falling to the Romans. Motives never change: conquer, defeat, control, defeat.

The first residents of Scotland to appear in history by name was Calgacus "the swordsman," a leader of the Caledonians at Mons Graupels, who was the most distinguished from birth and valor among the chieftains. Tacitus, a Roman statesman, even invented a speech for Calgacus in advance of the battle in which he describes the Romans:

> Robbers of the world, having by their universal plunder exhausted the land, they rifle the deep, if the enemy be rich, they are rapacious; if he be poor, they lust for domination. Neither the east nor the west has been able to satisfy them. Alone

among men they covet with equal eagerness poverty and riches to robbery, slaughter, plunder, they give the lying name of empire; they make a solitude and call it peace.

This excerpt from an all-powerful speech not only depicts truth from antiquity but also holds true today. Fallen man's basic instincts have never changed. "The heart is deceitful above all things, and desperately wicked: who can know it?" (Jeremiah 17:9, sixth century BC).

The Scots

The Scots are a determined, resilient people. After several more name changes, Scotland finally emerged the winner in the ninth century. Alba is Scottish Gaelic—English for *aelba*. They emerged from two Celtic-speaking people, the Picts and the Gales, who founded the kingdom of Scotland. The Scots and the Irish were traditional enemies for centuries, never seeing eye to eye on anything, especially religion. The Scots are Protestant, and the Irish are Catholic.

The Battle of the Boyne remains a controversial topic today in Northern Ireland. The Battle of the Boyne in 1690 was between the deposed king James VI of Scotland, attempting to regain the thrones of England and Scotland, and William VII of Scotland, who, with his wife, Queen Mary II, had acceded to the crown of England and Scotland in 1689. Wars never cease! Power struggles for wealth, power, and religious disagreements are alive and well today. Never forget that evil people will always be around fanning the fires of hatred and racism, spreading fear and disruption among the populace. These wicked forces are out in full bloom today. Can't miss it, just look around you.

In 1715 occurred the greatest Scotch and Irish exodus from Ulster, Ireland, to the Americas. During the American Revolution, the Scots were one sixth of the entire population of the Thirteen Colonies. In the war of independence, they were almost to the man on the side of the insurgents. Scots were twelve of the fifty-six signees of the Declaration of Independence, twelve delegates to the Constitutional Convention. These loyalists were all part of the birth of our nation.

The Scots and Irish were descent from a long, lean, powerful arm of the Union. They saved Kentucky from joining the South. The first sizable group of Scots to arrive in North Carolina as a body was the so-called Argyll of Western Scotland, who settled on the lower Little River. Our Hutchison clan does not fall in this category.

CHAPTER 4

My Hutchisons

Our third great grandfather, Robert Hutchison, was born in Scotland in 1775. James S. Hutchison Sr., our second great grandfather, was born in Ballymena, County Antrim, Northern Ireland, in January 1898. The family migrated to America around 1840 to Blackstock, Fairfield County, South Carolina. James S. Hutchison married Sarah Sallie Johnson (1796–1871) and had six children. Sarah and James married prior to coming to this country. He passed away at age sixty-four, on January 13, 1862 in Choctaw County, Mississippi, buried in Bethsalem Cemetery. Both Sarah Sally (1796–1871) and James Sr. are buried in Bethsalem Cemetery.

These are the children of Sarah Sally and James Sr., our second great grandfather: James Jr.; Robert (bachelor); Eliza (Stewart); Peggy (Brice), buried in Cherokee County, South Carolina; and Nan (Smiley). Nan was Jack Hutchison's mother. Jack was born out of wedlock. His father was a Johnston passing through during the Civil War. Our grandfather, John McCormick, raised Jack. John Hutchison was the youngest son who fought in the Civil War in the Fifteenth Mississippi Infantry. This John is buried at Bethsalem.

Our great grandfather, James S. Hutchison Jr. (1824–1884), was born in Winston County, Mississippi, and is buried in Bethsalem Cemetery. James Jr. married Sarah Henderson Wilson (1791–1877). They had nine children: John McCormick (1856-1936); Robert (Uncle Bob); William (Uncle Ben); Sarah Jane Kerr (a Bible scholar); Nanny (Nan) Griffin; Margaret Elizabeth Pickle (Aunt Lib); Martha (Aunt Mat), buried at Salem Methodist; Mary Campbell, Bethsalem Cemetery, married to Dr. Campbell, Sulphur Springs, Mississippi (more about this beastly, merciless man later.); Martha (Mat) Gladney, buried at Salem Methodist (Aunts Mat and Mary were twins); and Aner Harden (James), buried at Mt. Zion, Presbyterian in the Panhandle.

Our great-grandmother Sarah Henderson Wilson, 1827–1904, died in the home of John McCormick Hutchison. Sarah was the daughter of William and Margaret Elizabeth McCreight Wilson, buried at Bethsalem Cemetery. Sarah was related to President Woodrow Wilson. Not a big deal, especially since I abhor President Wilson's politics. The Wilsons moved to Columbia, South Carolina, in 1870 where they lived for around four years. This is when the Hutchisons, staunch Presbyterians, met the Wilsons. Woodrow's father was a prominent Presbyterian minister. He helped organize the Presbyterian Church of the Confederate States of America. The church leased slaves from slave owners rather than owning slaves, as was the custom. Wilson grew up around a majority African American community in Columbia, South Carolina.

In the early 1800s, South Carolina College was a significant institution in the growing city of Columbia. In order to understand slavery on campus, it is necessary to examine the role of slaves in Columbia during this era. Contrary to trendy belief, not all slaves lived on plantations. Urban slaves in Columbia typically lived and worked in close proximity with one another. Great distances often separated small communities of rural slaves.

In 1830, 1,500 slaves lived in Columbia; this population grew to 3,300 by 1860. Some worked in their masters' households. Masters also frequently hired out slaves to Columbia residents and institutions, including South Carolina College. Hired-out slaves sometimes returned to their owners; others boarded with their temporary masters. These relationships permitted communication among slaves and the city's small community of free Black people. Although various decrees established curfews and prohibited slaves from meeting and from learning to read and write, such rulings were difficult to enforce. Several prewar accounts note that many Columbia slaves were literate; some slaves even conducted classes to teach others to read and write. In spite of white efforts to prevent Black people from congregating, slaves and free Black people persevered to build a strong community of their own in Columbia.

Urban slaves participated in white organizations, though in limited roles, and attended services at local

Baptist, Presbyterian, and Methodist churches. Jack, a college slave, applied for membership in the First Presbyterian Church in April 1820. Church leaders postponed this decision for two years. Jack did not obtain membership before his death in 1822.

I maintain that Jesus knew Jack's heart; therefore, Jack is with the Lord despite the evil intentions of the so-called white Christians hindering his path. No religion or denomination on earth can save a person; salvation is from Jesus alone. Jack's story provides evidence of whites' utter discard for the contribution of slaves throughout this period. Just another horrible blot on our history. I also do not condone the methods put forth today by the liberal African American leaders. Prejudice toward Whites is no different than any prejudice toward anyone. My parents taught me that "two wrongs will never make a right." I very much doubt young Woodrow considered Black people his equal.

Woodrow Wilson was an enthusiastic proponent of the League of Nations, a peacekeeping organization established at the end of WWI, a foot in the door of socialism. Wilson, a Democrat, promoted the liberal movement in this country. The United States did not officially join the league due to opposition from isolationists in Congress. This was the beginning of the determined New World Order snarling and snapping at our freedoms today. World peace would be a glorious blessing, if possible, but world history paints quite a different picture.

Do not be fooled by phony statistics. As a whole, mankind's basic instincts have never changed. He is easily led around by the nose when appealing to his ego, his pocketbook, and most of all, his ignorance. We are headed at warp speed toward a one-world government. The Bible clearly speaks of this as well. America is bit by bit returning to the days of Roman and Greek culture, controlled by the elite—a dreadful thought!

CHAPTER 5

Mississippi

Our grandfather John McCormick Hutchison was born in Winnsboro, Fairfield, South Carolina, on July 11, 1856. All the Hutchison family left South Carolina and settled in Choctaw County, Mississippi, near the rural towns of Weir and Ackerman. He owned and operated a thousand plus acres of land in North Mississippi, where he farmed cotton among other things. This land once belonged to the Choctaw Indians, who were long gone by then.

Our grandfather's sister Mary Hutchison Campbell was married to Dr. Campbell from Sulfur Springs, Mississippi. They lived in the town of Weir. Mary often visited family alone either by horseback or horse and buggy. Word reached Grandfather that Dr. Campbell planned to murder Mary then sneak the body out of town by train. Dr. Campbell shot Mary and tried to hide the body on the train to Ackerman before anyone found out. There were two bodyguards on the train in charge of Mary's body.

Grandpa gathered up a posse, a mule, and a wagon then set out to stop the train, which he did. Ignoring the bodyguards, they took Mary's body off the train. Grandpa kept her body at home a few days then buried her in Bethsalem Cemetery. The despicable Dr. Campbell has never been heard of since.

John McCormick Hutchison married Florence Virginia Pollard. Our father, John Coyt, was one of eight children: Glover, Lillian, Willie, Lula, Montrose, John Coyt, Harvey, and Eppa, who lived one year. Lula married Virgil Rhodes. They owned and operated Rhodes Dairy in Bay Minette, Alabama, in early 1900s. I believe it is still in operation today. As a young girl, Lula's morning chore was milking two cows, unless prohibited by snow or frozen ground. Lula learned her trade early in life. She was killed in a car accident at age ninety-three, in perfect health and with all her faculties.

Aunt Lillian lived to be a hundred. She married Homer Fancher. Uncle Ho had connections with Billups of Billups Oil Co. Billups's first service station was in Carrolton, Mississippi. Aunt Lil was the first woman to attend college at French Camp. The first woman! Can you imagine? On her first day of college, Uncle Willie drove her the fifteen or twenty miles in a horse and buggy. One of the brothers continued to drive her each day. Would love to have been Aunt Lil that first day. Since my brain has been on fire from birth, I would have puffed up like an old toad. Knowing Aunt Lil, I'm sure she did. Her arrival surely drew a crowd of onlookers. Several Mississippi papers covered the event. All seven children were productive citizens.

The latest family member to claim the name Coyt is my great-grandson Coyt John Hamlin—the fifth Coyt. His mother, Marcy, is my granddaughter and my name-sake. The original spelling was Coit, which Daddy changed to Coyt. Truly a good Scottish name. A bit of trivia here: the site of the mythical King Arthur was a forest in what is now Scotland called Coit Celidon in early Welsh.

Our grandmother Florence Virginia Pollard Hutchison died a few days before her ninety-sixth birthday. At about ninety, while carrying a pale of ashes across the backyard, she fell and broke her hip. In those days, broken hips were tragic. Nothing to be done. Confined to a wheelchair for the remainder of her life, Grandma sat there, dipping her snuff until her death at ninety-three. She had a nasty make-shift spittoon made from a coffee can lined with paper. Hated that nasty thing! Sweet gum twigs chewed on one end until soft served as a brush for dipping. Since grandma had no teeth, we did the chewing. It was another different experience for me. Sometimes Virginia and I would pre-tend to dip snuff made of coco and sugar. Children's minds have never changed; they are like a giant sponge soaking up everything, unaware that habits may form before they real-ize. Never would snuff appeal to me, but the idea of doing my own thing was always an appealing thought. Grandma always said, "Marcia Nell is a torn-out piece."

The youth of Grandma's day patterned their dip-ping after somebody. You know the routine: "everybody's doing it." Thankfully, I only had to deal with cigarettes. Had my first cigarette stuck in the middle of my mouth, puffing away while swinging merrily across the creek on a vine. The trend has gone from snuff and alcohol to cigarettes to a selection of life-threatening drugs. With Cousin Louise, we pretended smoking rabbit tobacco (a stinking weed) wrapped with Uncle Willie's paper. Yuck! Once was enough; we nearly choked to death!

Aunt Montrose, the youngest daughter, faithfully cared for grandma till her death and everyone else as well. If there was such a thing as old folks' homes, I didn't hear about them. Christians took care of their own. Just being part of Aunt Montrose's daily routine, life lessons were deeply ingrained; learned the meaning of love, loyalty, and servanthood from her. With maturity, warm memories and feelings from our past will brighten any dreary day. Never before or since have I felt so safe and secure with anyone. It was just there in spades. Impressionable children will often overload. That's me! Sam Gordan Jones was a black man that lived on Grandpa's land his entire life. Aunt Montrose grew up with Sam; they were the same age. Sam was like family. When Sam Gordan wanted his pension, he had no proof of birth. So Aunt Montrose wrote Sam's name and birth date in the old Hutchison's Bible, and that was acceptable. Sam Gordan received his pension.

Camp Meeting

The mark of all Scots is their sense of identity with their dead, even to the twentieth generation. This certainly applies to our family. People may find this morbid, gloomy, or just plain silly. Family loyalty deeply ingrained in family history is passionately observed by our family. I find nothing morbid about honoring our ancestors that blazed a trailed before us.

Once a year, Bethsalem Cemetery is visited and tombstones discussed during camp meeting. This was an intricate part of my cherished childhood memories. Loved learning my ancestral history from elderly relatives and often from engraved tombstones. We have a Confederate soldier—Fifteenth Mississippi Infantry, Company A—buried at Bethsalem. I was so proud of that. There is a big contrast in the way the Hutchisons and the Lotts viewed their ancestors. After my mother's parents died, I only remember visiting their graves once or twice.

Everyone sat around the camp, enjoying the cool nights under a blanket of stars while moonbeams danced through the treetops. The riveting sounds of a gazillion chirping crickets permeated the air, especially in the graveyard's ghostly darkness. I was scared silly of ghosts coming up out of the ground to gobble me up. Can you imagine such bizarre thoughts? Only the very brave dare enter the graveyard after dark, and that was older cousins ready to play tricks on us. There was always someone around to dare you.

As for me, two or three times was enough. Call me a coward; see if I care. They talked about the dead all day long as if they were alive. So what was a little girl to think? It might have been funny to the adults, but I certainly wasn't amused. The limit to my bravery was occasionally running back and forth to the fence wailing like a banshee. Never a dull moment until closing our eyes at night. Not until I was grown did I learn what a banshee was. Banshee is an Irish legend, a female spirit whose wailing foretold an impending death in a house.

Camp meeting food was wonderful: all fresh veggies and fruits, freshly killed chicken and pork from the farm, homemade yeast rolls to die for, homemade ice cream and desserts galore. Food was prepared daily by the loving hands of faithful cooks, all the watermelon, cantaloupe, and veggies you could eat right from the fields.

There is a cool sand-bottom natural spring downhill from the tents that supplies the best tasting icy water in the world. Buckets filled with spring water were carried uphill daily. Watermelon and cantaloupe cooled perfectly when submerged in the spring. Years ago, our father built a cypress box to sit down into the ground containing the flow of water. The overflow gently trickled down hill resting in the little creek below. That cypress box will never rot; it will be there for eternity.

As very young girls, we sometimes, naked as jaybirds, put a log across the creek then perched there like birds chirping on a wire. Talk about fun! Talk about cold! Must not forget the outdoor toilet and the Sears-Roebuck catalog, quite handy for toilet paper. Then there was Choctaw Lake for swimming. How I miss those grand old days. Brother's family, along with many Hutchisons, still attend the yearly camp meeting reunion.

Here is a true testament to Scottish stubbornness. Our grandfather and his brother never agreed on the spelling of our name. We are the *-ison* and the other clan, *-inson*. The families are buried on either end of the same cemetery, Bethsalem Church, Choctaw County, Mississippi. Our parents and my youngest son, Lindsey, are buried there, and my sister and I will also be there. Hopefully, our brother and his family as well.

The original church was a log cabin built between 1839–40. Bethsalem is on the historical register; the grounds will always be maintained. In the early years, a circuit rider clergy traveled around, ministering to rural congregations. Once a year, our church holds a revival that lasts a week with two services a day. In the old days, travel on red clay roads with or without rain was hazardous by horse and buggy or wagon, so people pitched tents and stayed the entire week. When our grandfather came along, he built a large wooden tent downhill a bit from the church, with bed frames for mattresses. Camp meeting as I know it was born.

Since there was no flooring, sawdust covered the ground. There were two large front rooms with a large hallway between, and across the back was a long dining table, wooden benches on either side, and a kitchen with a wooden stove on the other end. Men slept on one side and women on the other. Oil lamps were our only source of light. By the time I came along, we had a nice wooden children's tent. I just loved sleeping with all my cousins four or five deep in a bed. As I was the youngest, all the foolishness was directed at me. Believe me I relished all the attention. Our little tent was full of fun, warmth, and love.

Summers at camp meeting will forever hold a special place in my heart. First Sunday in August is reunion day with a hundred plus relatives from everywhere attending.

Fun! Fun! Fun! To make me feel even more special, my birthday is August 2.

Grandma's House

We spent most summers in Mississippi and, on occasion, Christmas when I was very young. At Christmas, our uncles cut a pine tree from the woods behind the house. The decorations were mostly homemade ornaments, stringed popcorn, painted pine cones, shiny silver icicles, candy canes, and always a star on top.

Days of Innocence

Summers spent with my cousins Virginia, Eleanor, and Louise were like living in a fairy tale, intrigue always behind the next tree. These were the best years of my life. Virginia lived with Grandma, Eleanor lived down the lane through the pasture, and Louise several miles away across Telby Creek. Uncle Willie used to scare me to death talking about the black panther that lived in that creek and assured me that he sometimes slept in the cellar below our bedroom. I did not sleep a wink at that house. All three cousins were the same age, and then there was me, four years younger. They gave me a tough time, and I loved every moment of it.

Virginia had a playhouse full of dolls and anything else you could imagine playing with. Our playhouse community consisted of a yard full of cackling chickens, our neighbors on the left, the shower house on the right, and behind that was the pear orchid. Virginia got the first bicycle. This is where I learned to ride when my big toe barely touched the pedals. It's a wonder I survived that learning experience spending more time sprawled on the ground than riding. Finally declaring myself expert on wheels, I rode like a champ. My favorite thing was playing mail carrier, riding the bicycle all around, delivering mail to a bunch of cackling chickens and a few frenzied squirrels. Our playhouse had one little window with a flower box full of flowers that bloomed all summer. Yes, I captured this tranquil scene on canvas.

After a big breakfast, cooked on a wooden stove in the early days, we played hard till lunch, then out again till dark. Suppers were light. With a cool summer breeze drift-

YOU ONLY KNOW WHAT YOU KNOW

ing gently across our bed, we slept like logs. In the winter, after warming by the fire, we jumped in our cozy feather-bed. Each morning before we peeped, Uncle Bernice had another roaring fire going in our room. Central heat was unheard of in those days, only a cozy fireplace giving each room a pleasant ambience unsurpassed by central heat. As long as someone else was around to carry in the wood and remove the ashes, I would trade central heat for a cozy fire any day. Even now, I prefer my old floor furnace to central heat.

The playhouse sat along the side yard of the big house. There was a huge dinner bell on a wooden frame just off the back porch. I could hear Aunt Montrose now, "You girls stay away from that bell—it might fall on you!" The dinner bell rang at lunch time to call the men in from the fields. In case of emergency, called the neighbors.

The little playhouse at one time housed the workings for carbide lighting. Grandfather always up on the latest, installed the carbide lighting system throughout the house. Each room had a light fixture on the wall. Can you just imagine seeing such a thing bringing light into that big old house? Not for long! By the time I came along, only the fixtures remained. Back to the old faithful oil lamps.

There was a dirt floor smokehouse in the backyard where salty ham and sausage were cured. Meat hung on hooks above a slow-smoking fire for days, curing the meat. Told not to go in there, so naturally I did. How else was a curious little girl to understand the curing process unless seen with her own eyes. And later, I was inspired to paint the old smokehouse that sits behind the big house now belonging to our cousin.

The barn lot was downhill from the house. Cornfields right of the pasture supplied corn for the cattle. The barn had stalls on either side with a lane between and hay loft above. Anytime we entered the barn, I had to grind an ear corn through the handy grinder hanging on the wall. That grinder fascinated me. Outside, the lot was a deepwater well with a bucket and rope that supplied all the water necessary, except for human use. There were various other buildings on the place that housed equipment and one for cotton seed.

In the 1800s, cottonseed oil was primarily used in oil lamps and to make candles. Today, it's used in laundry detergent, insecticides, cosmetics, and numerous other uses.

Amy was the cook for as long as I can remember. She made the all-time best chicken and dumplings in the entire world and also long, flat fried apple pies to die for. Amy's daughter was one of my playmates. We spent hours under the house, twirling a little stick down a hole, yelling, "Doodle bug, doodle bug, come out your hole. Come out, come out. Your house is on fire." We twirled and whirled, yelling, "Doodle bug," until our fingers cramped. Then we fell out, laughing ourselves silly when doodle bug never showed up. We had such silly fun together. I just cannot recall her name. I dearly loved those innocent fun days.

Amy also had two sons: Brother (not too bright) and Rat Tail, who got himself killed in St. Louis. We never had contact with Black people at home, except the man who plowed up our garden every spring. These guys were my buddies, always under Montrose and Amy's watchful eye.

Brother's job was to make sure I didn't kill myself riding the mule, old Nell, or when adventure lured me into all sorts of mischief; faithful Brother's eyes were right on target, sometimes to pick up the pieces. On this day, I decided to ride Old Nell bareback, something I knew absolutely nothing about. Didn't let that stop me. A new and exciting adventure is always welcome. So at my insistence, Brother lifted me up, fussing all the time, "You're gonna fall. You're gonna fall."

With Brother on a mule behind me, we took off down and up the hill to the gin, then down a longer, steeper hill to a sand bed in the bottom. Well, the minute Nell hit that sand bed, she took off like a bat out of hell, leaving me behind, sprawled in hard, packed sand—not friendly to the back side. I just sat there in a daze until Brother caught up. After seeing I was in one piece, he went after Nell. A little straddle-legged girl hobbled along the walk back home. My bottom stayed sore for days. Cured me. I was never again curious about bareback riding. Don't you know!

Rat Tail drove me in the wagon to the watermelon patch, where we loaded up with sweet sun-ripened melons. Nothing like the luscious red heart ripened to perfection, especially eaten right in the field with juice running down your face. Rat Tail taught me how to tell when a melon was ripe by listening for a hollow sound while thumping the melon before picking it. We often picked field peas from the pea patch. I still enjoy field peas today. Sometimes, under Rat Tail's supervision, he let me hold the reigns. It was a little unnerving, but my tenacious spirit accepted the challenge. I felt so brave and privileged, and believe me, I was. Rat Tail convinced me he was really smart. So smart, he got himself killed in St. Louis.

Daddy built the shower house, a square bottom structure walled halfway up, then tapering to a platform above, where a barrel supplied water pumped in from a well—of course, a showerhead hanging down. Can you imagine the fun we had in that ice-cold water? Showers were only good in the summertime. By the time we got back to the house, we had sand all over our feet and legs. Dear Aunt Montrose faithfully greeted us on the back porch with towels. Winter baths were in a large wash pan filled with hot water, heated on the stove, and shared with Virginia. Occasionally, Montrose joined us. Virginia would say, "Here comes Trose. Rub a dub, dub, three men in a tub." A wonderful old nursery rhyme.

The cotton gin is seen from the side porch, past the orchard, down through the valley, through the cornfield, and sat atop the next hill. Our grandfather was a cotton farmer, among other things. He also ginned for the public, both black and white farmers alike. The ginning process fascinated my curious mind. Someone was always trying to run me out of the gin. Didn't work! Although I observed the operation from beginning to end, I wanted everything explained to me. Surely, I annoyed people at times, but someone always found patience enough to indulge me.

What really baffled me was the mules pulling a wagonload of cotton on the scales and know the weight of the cotton. I just couldn't understand how such a thing could work. Naturally, I couldn't rest without an explanation. For those who may not know, this is how the scale works. There was a scale underground covered with thick boards on top. The wagon pulled onto the scale, then the cotton sucked up in a big tube to the top of the gin, where the seeds were separated from the cotton. The difference in the wagon's weight gave you the weight of the cotton.

I remember peeping through the big cracks, trying to see the scale, and never did clearly see the thing. Surely was a noisy place when all those wheels were turning. Seems to me that hanging out in a cotton gin at six or seven years old is less threatening than the shopping malls of today. My aspirations were the antithesis of all the youths I knew back home. No way would I trade places with anyone then or now. Face it. I knew some stuff.

There was a blacksmith shop across the road from the big house full of all sorts of interesting things to discover. In later years, with camera in hand, I photographed everything in sight and often captured the moment on canvas. There was an old anvil iron in the blacksmith shop covered in yellow sawdust all aglow from sunlight beaming through the only window. No doubt, this was to be my next painting. The camera had captured the mood so beautifully that I was able to create a lovely oil painting. A man in Algeria, North Africa, owns this small painting. Regrettably, I neglected to get a photograph of the finished painting.

Sorghum cane molasses was made every year from sugarcane grown in the fields. A mule attached to a pole on one end and a grinder on the other walked round and round, grinding juice from the cane. Then the juice was boiled in a vat, constantly skimming foam off the top. Our uncles grew the cane and made the syrup. Nothing any better than biscuits, butter, and cane syrup. Daddy had biscuits or corn bread with molasses and butter every night after supper, whether we had dessert or not. Never failed to irritate Minnie Ola.

Grandfather even had his own sawmill, made his own lumber, trees cut from his own land. He also milled for the public. He owned a general store at Highpoint, a town of the very distance past. During the winter, when the farm was inactive, he made wooden caskets. Can you imagine? This is what you call true innovation. There was not a lazy bone in that man's body. A strong work ethic will never fail you. Later generations lack this all-important strength. Where do we place the blame? Can hear my mother now: "If the shoe fits, wear it." Grandfather drew his strength from the Bible, which he read every night. "Idle hands are the devil's workshop; idle lips are his mouthpiece; An evil man sows strife; gossip separates the best of friends" (Proverbs 16:27–28).

CHAPTER 6

A Louisiana Wedding

Our father graduated from Mississippi State and further studied in Nashville, Tennessee. Daddy's first school was Doyle, Louisiana, where he was principal. This was where my mother lived with her eight siblings. She was a senior student at that time. Sometime after graduation, Minnie Ola Lott married the principal. How long after, I do not know. Mother was quite bright, exceptionally beautiful, and fourteen years younger than my father. She only attended college for a couple of years.

Albany

Sometime later, Daddy transferred to another school in the small community of Albany, in southeast Louisiana. Albany had a large Hungarian population, where farmers raised strawberries. All rural schools' grades 1 through 12 were in the same building, schoolhouse. Daddy was the principal, taught senior math, and coached the basketball teams as he did in all the schools. Mother was scorekeeper for the ball games. My parents lived in a small apartment above the only drugstore in Albany. I was born in that apartment on August 2, 1934. Arrived in the wake of the depression. Society would not recover for years to come. In just ten short years, WWII would break out.

Interesting bit of trivia to note that the name Albany came from the capture of the Dutch New Netherland by the English in 1664. This was a seventeenth-century colony of the Dutch Republic found on what is now the east coast of the United States. The name changed from Beverwijk to Albany in honor of the Duke of Albany (later, James II of England and James VII of Scotland). The name is derived from Alba, the Gaelic name for Scotland. This is another perfect example of how great and evil men alike have constantly sacked towns, changed names, ravaged, and murdered—all for the glory of man's ego and greed. Man's belligerent attitude has altered the course of history since the beginning of time. Hopefully, this message will convey the ever-changing social phenomena we face today. "There is nothing new under the sun."

French Settlement

We moved from Albany to French Settlement, a Cajun French community on the bayou. Louisiana French refers to the complex of dialects and varieties of the French language spoken traditionally in south Louisiana. The depression changed everything. Daddy was a hardworking man. We never had a closet full of clothes, yet we never did without clothes or food. In fact, I was unaware that we were lacking anything. Since everybody was in the same boat, there was nothing to make a comparison.

For years, Mother made all our dresses. Never will forget how immensely proud I was at about age five when mother bought me a Shirley Temple dress. Wanted to sleep in it. It felt like I was wrapped up in a warm fluffy pink cloud like the kind I often dreamed of. I was one happy little girl having absolutely no concept of what my parents sacrificed to buy that dress for me. Just seeing my excitement was enough reward for them. It's certain no one reading this story can relate unless they are near my age and had a Shirley Temple dress.

My very favorite depression story was when Mother went to Kress on Third Street in Baton Rouge to buy buttons for a dress she had made. On tiptoes, barely able to see over the counter, I remember watching her carefully examine all the different buttons. After finally making her selection and ready to pay, she was two cents short of enough money to buy a fifteen-cent card of buttons. Can still hear the disappointment in her voice. Nothing to do but go home and try again another day. And that is what we did.

It is doubtful anyone could even imagine having to go home and save two more pennies to make a fifteen-cent purchase? I think not! We are a spoiled people; even the poorest among us are not hungry. Do not be so sure America will never be in this same situation once again. As a people, we no longer count our blessings. We count our money! We think nothing of overloading credit cards to buy what we want, not necessarily what we need. We do what we want when we want and on our own terms, often never looking back until we are drowning in a sea of debt or sinking into depression for one reason are another. As I have not always traveled the straight and narrow path, many mistakes occurred along the way. Praise God, my family was there to pick up the pieces with love and nonjudgmental support. Despite my wrong choices, I never overextended myself. I can still hear Daddy's cautioning voice: "Never enter a tunnel unless you can see light at the other end." Wisdom like this has long gone by the wayside. I venture to say that some people may not even get the *tunnel* message.

Bath time consisted of a large galvanized washtub filled with hot water heated on the stove. All the houses had huge cisterns with screened tops and faucets to draw water for daily use. Nothing any better than rainwater for washing hair leaving it sparkling like diamonds. One of our houses had a wonderful artesian flow well that gave us a cool natural water flowing constantly from a ground pipe. As a very young child, I enjoyed a cold drink right from the pipe. There was a large cypress trough collecting the flowing water. Under Mother's supervision, I was occasionally allowed to play in that trough full of ice-cold water.

The French people knew about artesian wells. The word *artesian* comes from the town of Artois in France, the old Roman city of Artesian, where the best-known flowing artesian wells were drilled in the Middle Ages. The level to which water will rise in tightly cased wells in artesian aquifers is called the potentiometric surface.

Our neighbors, the Matherne family, raised strawberries. Must say that I know what vine-ripened strawberries the size of a large lemon tastes like and have not enjoyed one since. I rarely eat the tasteless berries sold in supermarkets. Matherne had a huge strawberry field. After the harvest was over, we filled our baskets with the most beautiful, delicious red strawberries in the world. While in the fields, I ate myself silly. Mother always made an endless supply of strawberry preserves. Even after we later moved to Baton Rouge, Daddy had a couple rows of berries in his large vegetable garden. The name *straw* was from the rows of pine straw as a protective covering for the roots but allows air and moisture through. Mulched pine straw is also beneficial for other acidic soil loving plants. Felicia Matherne remained Mother's good friend.

The Biscuit Thief

One day, I went next door to Mathernes, looking for Mother. We always went in through the kitchen. Standing in the kitchen door, a plate full of mile high biscuits were staring down at me from atop the old safe. They were the biggest biscuits I had ever seen, calling my name with every mouthwatering step. Unable to resist the temptation, I climbed up on a chair and politely helped myself to a tasty biscuit then sat on the back steps, enjoying every morsel.

Matherne noticed the missing biscuit, and she also knew who got it.

That afternoon, Mother confronted me about the missing biscuit. Although I felt only a tinge of guilt, I had no problem confessing. In my young mind, I knew Matherne would have given me a biscuit had she been there. This was five-year-old logic. Mother explained there was no excuse for not asking permission first. That made sense, so I got it!

All the ladies of the quilting group went to Baton Rouge to see the movie *Gone with the Wind*. This was a big deal for these ladies. A wonderful movie about the South and the Civil War, every person in this country would benefit from this historical story, one of the most popular movies ever. It painted the pretty pictures and the ugly ones but told the truth. The watchdogs at HBO Max have long ago removed the movie and claim it's not banned, just temporarily removed. More racist lies and more absurdity! The book may be banned as well.

Not sure when, but we moved to another house in French Settlement on the same gravel road closer to the school. It was a newer house with running water. Still no bathroom, but we had a cistern and a slop jar. We also had our first electric refrigerator with large coils sitting on top. Before that, I can't remember. Only oil-fired cook stoves were available. Our new house sat back from the road with a fence out back to separate the yard from the pasture that ended at the swamp. Our neighbors were Willy Sydney's saloon on the left front near the road and the Catholic church on the right. Then across the road was Mr. Hebert's general store and post office, where the old men spent all day on the porch chewing, spitting, yapping, and of course, observing everything that took place at our house.

I did not play in the front yard. On one rare occasion when Grandma Hutchison was visiting and babysitting, I decided to test my will against hers. You might say I won, of sorts. It was pouring down rain that day, so I decided to take off all my clothes and put on my new transparent rain-coat. Ignoring Grandma's pleading I proceeded to march myself out front, giving the general store crowd a show. The old fuddy-duddies across the road suddenly perked up. I pretended to be a beautiful fairy, dancing through the rain while catching raindrops in the palms of my hand. "Quite a trip."

There was a pile of lumber in the yard that I suddenly decided to sit upon. I scurried over fairylike, sat down, and promptly put a rusty nail through the palm of my hand. The show was over. However, I knew the store crowd witnessed the incident and were yakking in French ninety miles an hour, not quite sure what happened. In that case, I chose to simply stroll slowly back in the house, pretending noth-ing had happened. I certainly didn't want to cry in front of Grandma either but couldn't hold back my tears. My par-ents arrived shortly after to find me crying and bleeding. Grandma was nervously wringing her hands over the whole ordeal. It's doubtful her eight children ever pulled such a stunt. Well maybe not!

Daddy immediately took me cross the river by ferry then on to the nearest town with a doctor for a tetanus shot. Mother asked why I was outside in the first place. "Wanted to fairy dance in the rain." It was the truth, and that satisfied them. The subject was closed. At age five, did that teach me a lesson? Not yet!

Willy Sidney's was a bar on one end, an open-air pavilion on the other end with benches all around and a wooden dance floor in the middle. The unending sounds of the jukebox permeated the air with *honky-tonk* music. On weekends, all the people from two to toothless poured into Willy Sidney's. Spectators occupied the benches around the dance floor, where *jitterbuggers* danced all afternoon and evening. One Sunday afternoon, my little brother and I were peeking through the fence, taking it all in. Daddy soon showed up behind his unsuspecting wayward children, saying, "What are you doing?" I jumped a mile high, and Johnny said, "We were just watching them didderbud."

On occasion, Willie Sidney's turned into a makeshift theater, my first experience with movies. We called it picture shows. A screen was set on one end of the dance floor with chairs in the middle. Usually, the movies were cowboys and Indians or cops and robbers. Now that I think about it, Indians were never portrayed in a favorable light, always vicious, savage killers out to scalp the good guys. This was definitely brainwashing tactics at work. Hollywood is still at it today.

After moving to Baton Rouge, movies became a weekly outing. Early in Elvis Presley's career, he appeared in person at our Paramount Theatre. Mother was not in the least impressed and said, "He will never make it." Elvis was the antithesis of anything we had ever heard. When people rigidly cling only to what they can see, hear, taste and feel, the mind is closed. Elvis had a soulful quality to his voice with a wide range that penetrated your soul. The magic of his beautiful baritone voice is unsurpassed by any other, especially his gospel renditions. Elvis grew up singing in the church, where he came from humble beginnings. Elvis was born in Tupelo, Mississippi, then the family moved to Memphis, Tennessee, when Elvis was thirteen years old. Along with my sister, we visited the little shotgun house that was his childhood home. Then years later, I was fortunate enough to see Elvis in concert with my son Lindsey, who was pleasantly surprised.

Our generation was definitely brainwashed with all the glitz and glamour portrayed on the silver screen. Half the female population fantasied a vicarious existence of beauty and glamour. I surely did. One local claim to fame was Dot Bourgeois as Elly May (Donna Douglas) in *The Beverly Hillbillies*. Among other things, she played opposite Elvis Presley in 1966's *Frankie and Johnny*. Praise God, I finally outgrew daydreaming of fame and fortune. This was just before I jumped from the frying pan into the fire.

This story of Daddy's paycheck is worth mentioning here. Mr. Hebert had the general store across the road from us—you know, the old men's watering hole. Daddy's salary as school principal was $100 a month. He always received the check, except he couldn't cash it. In time, he would get all his money, but for now the parish didn't have any money. Mr. Hebert would hold the check and give Daddy $85. Pretty strong interest. We needed the money to exist. Is this what you call extortion? Can you imagine $100 a month salary? Our father was an educated man. The common laborers must have worked for pennies. These were challenging times, although I was unaware. No doubt, our generations of spoiled, self-absorbed individuals deserve what befalls our nation. Not a happy thought.

Crawfishing

When it rained, the swamp flooded, bringing water close to our back fence. High water was time to go crawfishing. Mother split a stick of stove wood into several pieces, and these were our fishing poles. She tied a piece of heavy twine around one end of the stick and when ready to fish, tied a chunk of stinky meat on the other end of the twine for bait. The crawfish loved it. We had a little shallow flat-bottom boat to maneuver us around the swamp until Mother found a suitable stump to perch me on. She gave me a baited pole and a net for my catch.

After a lesson on crawfishing and safety, Mother and her friend took off into deeper water. No sooner had I dropped my pole in the water when four or more huge blue crawfish clustered around the bait. Trust me, this was quite a sight for my young eyes. I bravely shook them off as fast as I could into a cloth flower sack tied to my stump. Never once thought of my handy net. For a little six-year-old girl perched on a stump, this was quite an experience and one I shall never forget. I felt so grown up, brave, and immensely proud of myself—so far, so good.

That very experience instilled a valuable sense of responsibility that has never left me. This was truly a wonderful time of my life. Both my parents told me I could do anything I set my mind to. So I had no problem jumping on the fast track. They just forgot to explain all the pitfalls of the fast track.

The school had a Tom Thumb wedding where I was the bride. Lost my little wedding ring that day in the swamp, never expecting to find it in all that mud. A month or so later, when the water subsided, by some miracle, our neighbor found the ring. That ring stayed on my finger until it nearly attached permanently.

How would you feel about leaving your child perched on a stump in the swamp? I believe trust and knowing my intense sense of responsibility answers that question. Before leaving, Mother knew I was securely perched atop the stump, or she would have never left me there. If my parents said you can do this or that, then I did it. Trusted my parents in those days. Why not, it always worked. They knew very well my strengths and weaknesses and never failed to point them out. Taught from a very young age to never say I can't. Strike those words from your vocabulary. I tried my best, and that was all ever expected of me. In fact, they never mentioned the fast track. Do you know the story *The Little Engine That Could*, published in 1930? "Yes, I can, yes I can," said the little steam engine as it tugged and puffed up the hill. Loved that book. This story was read to me all the time. You say you can't or won't because there is a trusty machine nearby to do it for you or a pill for false courage or someone else doing it for you. Fortunately, I had none of that, only my parents to guide me, encourage me, and my strength of mind to try. My young brain was always working overtime.

Whose Toe Is It?

One of my favorite memories was when left in charge of my little brother while Mother went next door. Bear in mind, this is a take-charge seven-year-old attempting to give orders to an iron-will three-year-old. Johnny's big toe was securely bandaged. However, since I was in charge, I decided the bandage needed changing. Good luck!

Immediately, war erupted, big time. Johnny refused to let me even touch the toe. He forbid me to even look at it. After several rounds of insisting I was in charge, a determined look came across his face. He looked up at me and said, "Whose toe is it anyhow?" That ended the fracas. All through the years, when one of us said, "Whose toe is it?" we got the message. For the longest time I called my brother *Prince*, and that usually got a yes.

Lady

We had a milk cow named Lady that supplied us fresh milk topped with three or four inches of rich thick cream. So good in café au lait or on hot cereals, biscuits, or pancakes and syrup. Yum! This was mother's daily breakfast menu. She would let me taste the pancake batter and occasionally pretend to set the table when I could barely see over the top to observe everything in the kitchen. Mother was a hands-on parent in those days. There was always plenty of fresh butter, eggs, and vegetables from our garden. This was Daddy's department.

When Johnny was about two or three, he liked to sit in the feed trough while Daddy was milking Lady, our wide-eyed blond cow with two-inch lashes. Johnny felt so brave pushing lady's feed toward her big munching lips, then swiftly jerking his hand back. Brother can do most anything because our parents were great role models in those days. We may not have had any money, but we ate like kings and all we wanted. Life was good.

We also had a huge prize-winning sow I was scared to death of. There is a picture somewhere of brave little Johnny sitting on the sow's back. To each his own; I wasn't about to try that. Our sow eventually give us all the pork we could eat. Grandpa Lambert butchered our sow, made delicious andouille sausage, hogshead cheese, hams, pork chops. Mother loved cracklings made with slivers of fat still attached to the skin then deep fried in a large black iron pot filled with lard. Delicious! Nothing like what you might buy in the stores today.

CHAPTER 7

Basketball

Can anyone reading this story imagine themselves walking in my father's shoes? He held a full-time teaching job, was school administrator and basketball coach, and was full time keeping up with all the chores at home. Again, I say, good Scottish stock! I vaguely remember sitting on a bench behind the team where Mother was the scorekeeper. I can vaguely remember what the gym looked like.

Daddy was a student of the game of basketball, and he was a great coach. He had a good rapport with his players, understanding their strengths and weaknesses. He knew how to get the best out of people. His expertise led two winning state championship teams and one runner-up state champion.

Daddy coached my brother practically from birth. It paid off as Johnny got a scholarship to Mississippi State. In 1959, state won the SEC conference state championship of fourteen teams. This qualified the team to compete in the NCAA tournament, a great honor. They stood a good chance of winning. Unfortunately, our excitement suddenly took a nose dive. The governor refused to let them go because Black people would be playing in the NCAA tournament. Is this not unbelievable? Ignorance and prejudice prevented these young men from reaping the rewards of their labor. Depriving the team of the honor and glory of participating in national competition is beyond ignorance. It was this very attitude that hindered relations between Black people and whites for years. Praise God, my mother was not a prejudiced person and when necessary, voiced her beliefs. Daddy was not as adamant.

As a young boy, our father had severe scoliosis of the spine. Normally, he would have been over six feet tall but was only five three. Daddy had long arms and huge hands. Our father's disabilities never deprived him of competent physical, intellectual, or moral powers. He always displayed a tower of strength and confidence his entire life. Daddy's chest and back were constantly pushing on his internal organs, causing them to work triple time. Praise God, our father outlived his life expectancy by many years. He went to be with the Lord at sixty-seven. Amazing!

School Days

Having my father as principal for the first three years of school did have some drawbacks at times. Although I was extremely proud to be Prof's daughter, I did lack in close friendships. Looking back, I think the lack of real friends—or really none—played a big part in my social development. Will never forget one day after school, while waiting for Daddy, some senior boys asked if I could spell my name. Being a smart-alecky little girl craving the attention, I said, "Of course, I can!" They gave me a piece of white chalk and told me to write my name across the front door of the school. I promptly wrote Marcia Nell in script across the huge brown double doors in white letters.

Well, as planned, the principal was immediately informed. Daddy took me into his office, leaving the door slightly ajar, and gave me a couple of painless licks with a paddle while the contriving boys stood in the hall, taking it all in. Much too angry to cry. If looks could kill, the hall would have been full of dead bodies. Mother was furious! Nothing Daddy said was going to change that for sure. Daddy tried to explain that he had to set an example because of who I was. He honestly believed he was doing the right thing, and so it was for the right reason. Closing the door would not have served his purpose. Of course, the only thing in pain was my ego. It did take a few years to understand that the boys were really testing my dad. They knew what I would do. Chalk that up to another of life's experience. No more white chalk on a brown door for me.

At recess, I would often befriend an extremely poor girl, who was an outcast because she was dirty, not very bright, and dressed in rags. The children were not very nice to her. It amazes me still that people can be so cruel. I did attempt to acknowledge her presence by occasionally hanging out with her, having conversation, something she rarely experienced outside her parents. She was mostly ignored at school.

Naturally, in her eyes, she thought I was wonderful. My parents taught me to always treat other people like I wanted to be treated, so I did and do! I never catered to the so-called snooty crowd. She lived with her family on the river in an old rickety houseboat. They were very poor and undernourished. Daddy always made sure she had lunch. Mr. Roland's store with one gasoline pump was right next door to the school; he made delicious canned meat sandwiches. Daddy often fed this child at Mr. Roland's store.

While we were in the second grade, the girl and her family contracted typhoid fever from drinking swamp water contaminated with all sorts of bacteria. The school immediately shut down all water fountains. We may have gotten shots; can't remember. After the family received medical treatment, they were quarantined for a period of time. Unfortunately, not much changed in their lives. I felt so sorry for my friend. I just cannot seem to remember her name, but I have never forgotten her little round freckled face and crooked teeth. We were around seven at the time. Surely, the empathy I felt for my little friend was a gift from God. The Lord blessed me with an empathetic spirit and, when acting on my own initiative, brought about most of my troubles. That's life. I'm not perfect, but I'm perfectly me.

My second and third grades were in the same classroom, rows side by side with the same teacher, as was the case in small rural schools. Ms. Althea Johnson was our teacher and my all-time favorite. Do you think I felt privileged? I even spent the weekend with her and her mother, who lived in another little town. The first morning, she served me a little glass of orange juice with breakfast. Not being quite sure if it were meant for me, I chose to ignore the situation. Ms. Johnson asked me why I had not drunk my orange juice. There was no way to avoid her question, so I said I didn't care for it. Certainly not going to tell Ms. Johnson that we never had orange juice at home, or that I was not sure what it was. Sometimes, we do recall the strangest things. At seven years old, it was my first embarrassing moment. However, I soon got past that uncomfortable feeling.

We lived in yet another house in French Settlement. Our neighbors were the Lamberts. I think this was before Mr. Hebert's store. They farmed and raised strawberries for market. Mr. Lambert was also a butcher. Every season, Mother worked in his packing sheds, packing and stemming strawberries for pennies a pint, which he sold at market. Selling berries with the stems removed wouldn't be allowed today. The extra money was welcomed. The children in these parishes started school a month earlier than other school in south Louisiana so they could pick berries. The family unit was extraordinarily strong among the French people in our community. Children were taught a proper work ethic—sadly, mostly missing in our societies today.

The Lamberts' house was made of wide cypress boards with shutters on all the windows with no panes or screens. There was a wood stove in the little kitchen and a large window with shutters that served to throw out dishwater or anything else the chickens might like. Grandma Lambert made a little loaf of bread every day, rising on the back of the stove. Any time I visited, Grandma gave me a piece of her bread with a little syrup. So good! One thing that stuck in my mind was the silver dinner knife that Grandpa had sharpened to a narrow blade. This was used to chop everything. Grandma didn't speak a word of English. Her pleasant smile said it all.

A roughly hewn cypress picket fence divided our yard from the Lamberts'. Ms. Regent's bedroom (one of the daughters), was up the steps in the rear of the house. Houses were built high off the ground necessary for air circulation and high water. No screens. All the beds had mosquito nets attached on top then let down on all sides at night. Yes, nets were essential as a protective cover from swarms of blood-thirsty mosquitoes. Mosquitoes flourished in the lowland swamps. When my brother was two or three, he would get up in the middle of the night, climb through the fence somehow, cross the yard, and climb very steep steps, then crawl into bed with Ms. Regent. Maybe he liked sleeping under the mosquito net. Who knows? Grandpa Lambert, for fear of Johnny hurting himself, removed the bottom rusty nails from one of the pickets so he could cross over by just pushing aside the picket. Soon, little three-year-old Johnny learned the ropes and continued his midnight journey much easier and safer.

Soon, our tranquil life will be gone: gravel roads, Willie Sydney's, grumpy old men at Mr. Hebert's store, the swamp—all things of the past I had grown to understand and love. This was a much kinder, gentler time in my life when our family was still firmly intact. Our Nation was slowly recovering from the Great Depression. When we moved to Baton Rouge, I did not easily adjust to Mother working away from home. If she wasn't in eyesight, she was always in hearing distance. There is no substitute for a mother. She was my best friend, my advocate, and my confidant for as long as she lived.

CHAPTER 8

Baton Rouge

Our family moved to Baton Rouge when I was eight and the middle of the third grade. We bought two gravel-road lots on the outskirts of town. Daddy's brothers came from Mississippi to help build our very first house. A nephew owned a lumber mill in Mississippi furnished the lumber. The house cost all of $3,000. Daddy got a little raise, and before long, Mother went to work. This was the way people helped family and neighbors in those days. So proud of that house. For the first time, I had my own room with a tester (canopy) bed and vanity covered in pink and green chintz and a little chest that I still use today. Mother loved pretty things, and before long, our home began to have nice things. We finally had our first real dining room with nice dining room furniture.

I arrived in this world at the end of the great depression of the 1930s. Both my parents, as products of the depression, were frugal almost to a fault. They raised us to count our blessings and never to waste anything, especially food. Grace was always said before every meal. We learned to value what we had because it might be the last. We were to respect nature, our surroundings, our country, the animal kingdom, our parents, other people, and their property. It was drilled into my head that many children in the world had no food, not even a roof over their head. This was the case throughout war-torn Europe at that time. Pictures of starving children would sometimes flash before my eyes. We were not given the privilege to refuse food we may not care for. No, eat what was on your plate and be grateful for it. You dare not address adults other than Mr. and Ms. It irritated me when this custom was tagged strictly as an ignorant Southern expression. It was our way of showing respect. The Northerners just didn't get it. These lessons are among those long-forgotten. Respect is a foreign language today. Both parents and society are to blame for our spoiled, self-centered youth.

At about nine, when my cousin Nell was visiting, I decided to take advantage of the situation and show off a bit. We were having liver for supper, and I absolutely hated liver and fried tripe, which we had once a month. Tripe was cow's stomach and came in a can. Yuck! Asked to say grace this *liver* night, I proceeded to ask God to bless all our food, except for the liver. This wasn't exactly planned; it just blurted out.

Suddenly, dead silence came over the table, except for Nell, who couldn't stop laughing. Everyone else was stunned. As for me, I was very pleased. Nell related the story to the entire family, and to this day, I have never lived it down. My beautiful Persian cat named Pinky always waited under my bench for her little snacks. She was especially fond of liver, and I gave her plenty of it. Starving children in Europe never crossed my mind, only getting rid of the hideous liver bit by bit.

CHAPTER 9

My WWII Experience

I recall WWII very well as I was ten years old. One afternoon, while lying on the floor, listening to *Terry and the Pirates* on my little radio, the station interrupted to say Japan had bombed Pearl Harbor. This had happened much earlier in the morning. We had no other source of news in the house, and both parents were gone. I didn't completely grasp the depth of the situation. I just knew this was terrible news.

Our entire nation immediately went to bat in defense of our country, the lives lost, and the destruction of our navy. This was the dawn of WWII and the beginning of national pride and sacrifice for the war effort. Every young man of draft age was called into service. Men and women of all ages volunteered for some branch of the armed forces. This was a time in our history when citizens loved our country and cherished our freedoms enough to die for them. This is when our women first entered the work force full-time, replacing the men. The stay-at-home mom has now become a thing of the distant past. Women went to work in the factories, building everything necessary for the war effort. Women joined the armed services as nurses, drivers, or wherever needed. Despite the best of intensions, this was the beginning of the family breakdown.

Grammar schools had paper drives—newspapers and magazines used for packing around equipment and weapons. We collected scrap metal necessary to recycle and make into bombs. Engine grease was also saved. All children had a part to play by collecting paper goods and scrap metal. Our auditorium was filled with paper goods to be bundled and weighed for pick up. As a sixth grader, I loved the times I was called to bundle and weigh paper in the auditorium. This is where I was when Daddy came to tell me we had a twin brother and sister. Our baby brother only lived a few hours. He died of an enlarged thymus gland. Mother let me name him Gerald after my friend Gerald Batt. Today's technology would have saved his life.

There was no television. We had newsreels in the theaters showing all the latest war news from Europe. We saw Hitler's death camps firsthand once a week. We could also keep up with the war in the Pacific

Paul Wayne and William Bryan Hutchison, cousins, joined the navy together. They were stationed on the *Wasp* at Guadalcanal, one of the Solomon Islands in the South Pacific, when the Japanese bombed their ship. They both jumped into the burning water, clinging to a kapok mattress found floating in the ocean. Kapok was the material that filled life jackets. They had only one life jacket between them. William Bryan said, "We are going to drown right here."

Paul Wayne, clinging to the mattress, said, "No, we are not. God is going to save us." Now that's real faith. He knew in his heart that God would rescue them.

After clinging to the mattress all day, they spotted a PT boat that finally rescued them at dusk. Our family knew the *Wasp* had sunk but had no news of survivors for a long time. There were tears, prayers, and faith that the Lord would bring our cousins home safely. He did.

The five Sullivan brothers enlisted in the US Navy on January 3, 1942 with the stipulation that they serve together. The navy had a policy of separating siblings but not strictly enforced. All five assigned to the light cruiser USS *Juneau*. Early in the morning of November 13, 1942, during the Battle of Guadalcanal, the *Juneau*, struck by a Japanese torpedo, was forced to withdraw.

Later that day, as the *Juneau* was leaving the Solomon Islands area for the other surviving US warships, the *Juneau* was struck again, this time from the Japanese submarine I-26. The torpedo hit the thinly armored light cruiser at or near the ammunition magazines, and the ship exploded and quickly sank. Aircraft and ships searched for survivors. One hundred of *Juneau's* crew survived the torpedo attack. All five of the Sullivan brothers died. After recalling this tragedy, I was able to get a more accurate account of the *Juneau* and the Sullivan brothers from *Wikipedia*. It is difficult to understand how a family ever survived the tragic loss of all their sons. *The Fighting Sullivans* was a movie chronicling the story of the brothers who sacrificed everything to remain united. I saw the movie.

When true stories like this and others are forgotten or deliberately shelved to hide the truth, it makes me want to set fire to every screaming liberal out there tearing down our country and challenging our freedoms. This true story is just one more example of destroying our history and for dumbing down our youth through the media and academia. If the truth wasn't detrimental to their lies, then why fear the past when brave men of honor sacrificed their lives to save our nation from evil empires? America was not the enemy.

President Harry Truman ended the Pacific war. Truman was the first and last sensible Democrat. On the morning of August 6,1945, the American B-29 bomber dropped the world's first atom bomb over the city of Hiroshima. Truman wrote, "It is an awful responsibility that has come to us." America did not seek to destroy Japanese culture or people; the goal was to destroy Japan's ability to make war. Praise God, it worked.

Aunt Lula's sons and one uncle on Mother's side served in WWII. Uncle Doug, a paratrooper, was killed jumping over Normandy; he's buried in this area of Northern France. Sweet cousin Doug never knew his father. On June 6, 1944, D-Day, the allied forces of Britain, America, Canada, and France attacked German forces on the coast of Normandy with a huge force of over 150,000 soldiers. The allied attack gained a victory that became the turning point for WWII in Europe.

CHAPTER 10

World Wars I and II

As a young girl, I lived through WWII. I vividly remember Hitler's evil plans very well and how our nation was changed in a matter of hours. Our once-peaceful existence faded away as the threat of impending war raged through the hearts and minds of our people. This could happen in America at any given time. It happened in the '60s while sleeping parents were doing their own thing, including me. Open your minds. Share with me the history of two world wars and the evils of Adolph Hitler, who changed the course of history—therefore, mankind's destiny. Our history! Our lives!

Evil Epitomized

WWI, also known as the Great War, began in 1914 after the assassination of Archduke Franz Ferdinand of

Austria and his wife, Sophie. While on an official visit to Sarajevo to inspect imperial troops, they narrowly escaped death. A Serbian terrorist threw a bomb at their open top car and missed. Later that day, they were not so lucky. After taking a wrong turn, a nineteen-year-old Serbian nationalist shot and killed them both. The killer didn't just happen to be there. Obviously, the wrong turn was deliberately planned if the first attempt failed. There were other assassins stationed along the way. What driver in his position and responsibilities would dare accidentally take a wrong turn? I'm not buying it. The Serbs knew their action would bring about war. Now both Germany and Austria-Hungary declared war on Serbia. Then Germany declared war on Russia, Serbia's ally, and then invaded France via Belgium, which caused Britain to declare war on Germany. This reminds me of a Three Stooges skit, "Who's on first?" This ridiculous fracas was the start of WWI. I question all their sanity. Other than evil, greedy minds seeking control, who would advocate wars?

By the time the war was over and the Allied powers claimed victory, more than fifteen million people, soldiers and civilians alike, were dead. Was the archduke's life, his pride worth more than fifteen million dead people? I hardly think so! Anger, coupled with pride and ignorance, is the culprit that causes people to make irrational decisions; it applies to personal relationships as well. Really, these countries just liked to war.

The masses rarely realize they are called to promote egotistical tyrants' agendas and greed—too brainwashed, hungry for a fight. Assuming they were paid, these narcissistic idiots just like to war no matter the suffering victims. Germany and its Allies were known as the Central Powers: Germany and Austrian-Hungary, later joined by the Ottoman Empire (Turkey plus the Middle East) and Bulgaria. Then Italy threw Austria under the bus, changing sides in 1915, and declared war on Austria and Hungary. Playing checkers with empires in the midst of battle. Think about that curious move.

No matter the pedigree or the vulgar billionaires hanging around watering at the mouth, they all seek power. Then once again, powerful men will alter the course of history with unbridled violence and bloodshed. Just like the Serbs, millions of dead bodies left in their wake are of no consequence to them. The little men in the trenches are nothing more than pawns on the world stage left bleeding and desolate. Today's conflicts are no different; it's all about power and control. I cannot point out this universal truth enough. *Wake up!*

When the war ended, a torrent of Russian forces poured into Germany from the east, and it became an orgy of rape and murder. One man shot then fed to the pigs, all this violence egged on by several Soviet propagandists fanning the fires of hatred and revenge, was the equivalence of another malignancy. Please, never forget the communists never let a crisis go to waste. Evil never rests! People are far too gullible for their own good. Stand tall at a distance, open your eyes, and observe.

Shortly after Obama won the 2008 presidential election, his chief of staff, Rahm Emanuel, spoke at a *Wall Street Journal* CEO conference. As the economic/financial crisis was unfolding, he said, "You never want a serious crisis to go to waste. This is an opportunity to do things that you could not do before." These words are directly out of the communist playbook. It is abundantly clear that Rahm Emanuel was not the first to use these words. Few gullible Americans will relate to these words or have even heard them. This is confirmation that Democrats will take advantage of the people and the country during times of crisis, crisis they created in order to push through radical left-wing policies that under normal circumstances most people would consider extreme and overreaching. Most likely, COVID was deliberately circulated throughout the world to give evil forces a much-needed crisis. True or not true, "There is nothing new under the sun." This should be abundantly clear to the astute mind. If it wasn't deliberate, then it was accidental and denied. This scenario is what they would like to have us believe. I'm not buying the lies put forth by the media.

Revenge is justice with teeth, which causes more problems than it can ever solve. Saber-rattlers will never pass up an opportunity to fan the fires of hatred before a naive world. Learn to think for yourself with an open mind. The truth will find you. "Do unto others as you would have them do unto you." The Golden Rule written on our rulers when I was a girl as a constant reminder to be kind. This was a good thing. Why is it gone today? Jesus gave us the Golden Rule, and He described it as the second greatest commandment. Of course, these words would never fit the liberal playbook or pass their lips. The Golden Rule, expeditiously removed.

After WWI, Germany faced one of the greatest economic challenges: hyperinflation. War debts and reparations drained the coffers. The German government could not pay its debts. Former allies disbelieved that claim. French and Belgium troops occupied Germany's main industrial area, determined to get their reparation payments.

In response, the Weimar government simply printed more worthless money. This backfired in a big way. The effort devalued the mark, and inflation increased. The cost of living rose rapidly, and people lost all they had. The country soon crumbled, and the people fell into petty thievery. They established an underground bartering system to help meet their basic needs. Mankind's instinct for survival is God-inspired. Use the inspiration in a godly way or forfeit to Satan. Will this be the new America?

When I think of Germany's situation, it rings painfully close to home. Only God knows if we will ever get out of debt or what befalls our nation of misguided people in this present climate of unrest. The US Treasury has been printing money for quite some time. Now, inflation is here. Germany's World War I debt was so crushing, it took ninety-two years to pay off. During the period of reparations, Germany received between twenty-seven and thirty-eight billion marks in loans. By 1931, German foreign debt stood at 21.514 billion mark; the main sources of aid were the United States, Britain, the Netherlands, and Switzerland.

When the smoke cleared after the war, desperate people were still desperate. Cannot say this enough. After WWI, Germany's feathers were singed and ready for the plucking. A waiting, scheming Adolph Hitler moved right in for the kill. Now the vulnerable German people were too easily influenced. They swallowed Hitler's propaganda: hook, line, and sinker. As a whole, humans are basically uninformed and painfully gullible. Pride is the culprit that kills.

The rise of Adolph Hitler began in 1919 when he joined the political party, the Deutsche Arbeiterpartei—the Government Workers Party, changed in 1920 to the National Socialist Government Workers Party, commonly known as the Nazi Party. What a mouthful! It was anti-Marxist, opposed to the Democratic Weimar Republic, and the Treaty of Versailles. Hitler advocated extreme nationalism, the unification of all German-speaking peoples, and noxious anti-Semitism. Hitler attained power in 1933 as chancellor by parliamentary election and backroom intrigue. This assured Hitler would constitutionally exercise dictatorial powers without legal objection. By hook or crook, the slimy worm finally obtained his goal

Adolph Hitler's New Order (ring a bell?) was the political order that Nazi Germany wanted to impose on the conquered areas under its dominion. Burrrrr, these words are too familiar. Hitler aimed to eliminate Jews then begin a New Order. He convinced himself the Jews controlled the governments of Russia, United Kingdom, and the United States. He decided that dehumanizing the enemy allowed German soldiers and officers to agree with the Nazi's new vision of warfare.

How could any intelligent person adhere to such egregious ideas? Just think: today, it's Christians who will be under the threat of elimination. Can't kill us all! Gullible young German soldiers were taught that Russians and Jews were nothing but animals. Grant them no mercy. What happened to their brains? Were their hearts dead as well? Killed, I say.

No matter how desperate, it's frightening to think how nearly an entire nation could so easily embrace such hideous, insane lies, much less put them into practice. This is the equivalent of ancient empires. Evil intentions give rise to corruption and unrest then spreads like wildfire through a guileless society. Let me assure you that all my senses are wide open and running on all cylinders. My brain has been on fire since birth. It's past time putting it to clever use. The gorilla is out of the cage. Well, maybe a big-mouth bird.

Germany was now in a very grave situation. This rings painfully close to home. President Trump is not responsible for our debt—quite the contrary. Remember, when the smoke clears desperate people are still desperate. Germany's singed feathers were now ripe for the plucking. Are we? Hitler was now ready for the kill, or so he thought. Defying or lying about Almighty God is stupid beyond words. No one but no one in denial will escape God's wrath.

What did Hitler accomplish other than a few years of murder, mayhem, total failure as a leader and as a human being? His poison easily betrayed an already desperate nation. The answer to that is, desperate or not, never ever allow yourself to fall into that trap.

World War II

As WWII was during my youth, it is important that people understand how Adolph Hitler affected our daily lives and why. Some of this I have already covered. Hitler was just one of other evil madmen in the bloody history of our world, all in search of world dominance. May I remind you of The New Order from 1933 to 1945. In just two years, Adolph Hitler transformed Germany into a dictatorship, autocracy. Still gives me the creeps. Nazism is a form of fascism with disdain for liberal democracy. Hitler embraced nationalism, anti-Semitism, racial hierarchy, and social Darwinism. His goal was to create a German homogeneous society based on racial purity. Anything else would be inferior.

This idiot surely read his press clippings every morning before breakfast—sweet marmalade for toast. Cannot wrap my head around this insanity. Today, it's all about racial conformity—spine-chilling. It's all about mankind's search for power and glory; no other reason. I remember discussing Hitler's worldview with my daddy when I was ten or eleven. Our talks were sometimes a bit unnerving because of the visual images racing through my mind. We only know what we know,

Let's define just one of Hitler's insane thoughts: social Darwinism. Survival of the fittest: the idea that certain people become powerful in society because they are innately better. Really, a better piece of what, a slimy worm? The earthworm squirm when cut in half. The half with a brain will grow into a full worm. Chop up a three-banded panther worm in half or thirds, and within eight days, you'll have separate functioning worms. This is why I often refer evil men to slimy worms. There has been an abundance of these worms working overtime through the world since its inception. Put one down and another takes its place. "Survival of the fittest."

This is a big fat absurd lie! Country folks call it *hogwash*. As a young girl, I remember asking my father who would be the fittest. Social Darwinism has attempted to justify imperialism, racism, eugenics, and social inequality. Once Daddy explained in simpler words, I only partially understood and tried to never look down on anyone. Today, these same insanities are imposed upon our youth, camouflaged with racism or anything else that serves the purpose. Think about it! The rich intellectual elite must surely believe they are superior beings, lording over us uninformed, ignorant peasants. Hitler did; they will try.

The Nazi Party won the popular vote in 1932. After the tyrannical little despot finally achieved absolute rule in 1933, he trounced over the German society like an angry runaway bull. Citizenship was denied those of Jewish descent. Hitler was a Jew who hated Jews. Go figure!

True to form, people in utter despair will lose all hope in everything, believe anything, and vote for anything. Remember, Germany just came out of WWI. The herd mentality will infect desperate people every time. Despondency is not the only culprit. Self-centeredness, the uninformed, and vulnerable youth are mostly ready to join up. Youth has always been ripe for the plucking, ready and willing to embrace any unorthodox ideas spewing out change. People will accept anything promising personal peace and affluence, whether true or not.

Too trusting for me. After climbing too many fences, I am convinced "the pasture is not greener on the other side." America, stay alert! Century-old tactics are used on unsuspecting societies this very moment. Our citizens are programed daily with chaos and lies flowing freely through liberal media, all on the take from George Soros. Criminals takes the side of criminals. Ruthless men have slowly been prying open America's doors with Nazism's extreme racist, authoritarian views and behavior, all under the umbrella of *equality*.

My black brothers, don't kid yourselves; you will never be equals, unless of course you have trillions of dollars to buy your way in, and not even then. The language may change, but evil intent is always the same. The world's view of equality is a lie, as proven throughout antiquity. Trust me, the populist will never be considered equal to the ruling class. Once our constitution is abolished, it will be too late. Our rights as citizens, our freedoms will have vanished. Wake up, people! We are all equal in the eyes of God, not the government nor any other entity vying for control. Once in control, they will pour acid in our wounds.

The Holocaust

Hitler, an egomaniac, believed the Holocaust would elevate his fame. Hitler was all about *self*. What a disgusting, horribly stupid little worm of a man. The Holocaust was the WWII genocide of six million Jews between 1941 to 1945—six million human beings. Nazi Germany operated death camps in central Europe to systematically murder over 2.7 million Jews. People were herded like cattle onto locked freight cars, then taken away to the slaughter. The victims either died in gas chambers, from doctors experimenting on live prisoners, or fell before a firing squad.

I personally saw newsreels in our theaters once a week of this operation, the death camps, and the mass graves. This was a time when the press was on the side of truth and righteousness and not propagandist, selling lies that serve a particular point of view, detrimental to our government and its people. The liberal press no longer reports the news today; they are paid propagandists creating news. True history may be disappearing, but enough truthful, factual reporting is still out there. Tune in before it's snuffed out forever. Take a stand for righteousness!

While living in Baton Rouge at about eleven, we crossed the Mississippi river by ferry then down the levee to Port Allen, where there was a German prisoner camp along the river. These guys had it great. They were fed, housed, and everything was clean and comfortable. It was a beautiful Sunday afternoon, and the prisoners were playing cards on picnic tables while soaking up sun. Of course, I had to wave, and much to my surprise, most waved back. We are all human beings created in the image of God. I recall Daddy saying, "They are so young to believe Hitler's madness."

Mother replied, "Youth can't see the forest for the trees."

I didn't get it at the time, but I've never forgotten that moment on the River Road in Plaquemines Parish, Louisiana.

The German SS were Hitler's henchmen. Initiated by the SS in order to eliminate "life unworthy of life," they murdered people whom they deemed had no right to life. Evil was playing God much like what we witness today in our streets and from our sinister politicians. German doctors used euthanasia programs against homosexuals and hospital patients with mental and physical disabilities, executed by programmer Adolph Eichmann. My father's physical disabilities would have meant his death, "life unworthy of life." Grandsons, you and yours would have never existed. Think about that.

After Germany's defeat, Adolph Hitler hiding in his underground bunker, the little coward took cyanide pills then shot himself in the head, along with his silly girlfriend. Adolph Hitler will surely spend eternity burning in hell as payment for his evil deeds. Hell is a real place God has prepared for the devil and his advocates. Denying hell exists will never invalidate this truth. This brief synopsis of German WWII history exposes man's inhumanity to man and the pitfalls of human ignorance, greed, and selfishness.

Benito Mussolini

Italy, 1922–1943. Another egotistical idiot making an ass of himself. Early in the twentieth century, Italy fought alongside Germany in WWII. Mussolini was a fascist.

Fascism: far right authoritarian, ultranationalism, dictatorial power, forcible suppression of opposition. Mussolini was an evil worm.

Forcible rings my bell. When opposing views posted on social media are deemed inappropriate, you are just simply snuffed out, insulting our First Amendment. Is this freedom of speech? Why would Americans ever succumb to dictatorial powers is a mystery to me. Our forefathers, imperfect as they were, left all that garbage behind in Europe. They feared loss of freedom and their life. Strict obedience to any authority at the expense of my personal freedom is unacceptable.

The uninformed, the ignorant, the rabble-rousers—all vulnerable and susceptible to never-ending subtleties of suggestions, pecking away at the brain, if they have one? Obviously, oblivious as to what the eyes see, and ears hear. What is that called, a doofus? Question everything proposed by the worms as fact, then earnestly search out the real facts. There is a saying, 'Believe nothing you hear and only half of what you see." Good advice. Remember, "you only know what you know." It doesn't take a mental giant to see that America is lied to, up one side and down the other. America and its people are not perfect, but we are the best there is in this world. Good common sense is the best path to sound wisdom.

CHAPTER 11

Milano

When my daughter Patricia lived in Milano (Milan), Italy, I spent several months there with her family. We visited many historical sites, including the painting of *The Last Supper* housed on a theater stage in Milano. Japanese artists were restoring the huge painting that nearly covered the width of the stage. Seeing only small photos of the painting, often on the back of a fan, the size surprised me. This painting lives as a reminder to the world of Jesus's final meal shared with His disciples before His crucifixion. During the meal, Jesus predicts his betrayal by one of the disciples present, Judas Iscariot. In 1494, Ludovico Sforza, duke of Milan, commissioned Leonardo da Vinci to paint *The Last Supper*. The work took years to complete and attempts to salvage it has taken centuries. I will forever be grateful to Patricia for this amazing experience as a believer and for inspiring my much alive art spirit.

While in Milano, we visited the site where the Italian people dragged Mussolini and his girlfriend's dead bodies around a little circle until only shreds of humanity remained. Earlier, their bodies had already suffered roadside execution. The Italian people knew no mercy as their anger had reached the height of bitter hatred.

As I stood in that place of history, I felt more than a little eerie. Sounds brutal; it was! This is when hate, livid with anger, fuels the fires of revenge beyond our control, a dangerous place to be. Having never walked in their shoes, far be it from me to judge. "Vengeance is mine, I will repay, says the Lord" (Deuteronomy 32:35, Romans 12:19, Hebrews 10:30). Do not avenge yourself. Benito Mussolini was a real worm. He was an Italian politician and journalist who founded and led the National Fascist Party. He was the fascist dictator of Italy for twenty years from 1925 to 1945. Originally a revolutionary socialist, he forged the paramilitary socialist movement in 1919 and became prime minister in 1922.

Mussolini, strutting around like a peacock, gradually dismantled the institutions of democratic government and in 1925 made himself dictator, taking the title *il Duce*. He attempted to reestablish Italy as a great European power. The regime held together by strong state control and Mussolini's cult of personality. Throughout history, all anarchists are nothing more than self-proclaimed dictatorial buffoons. Socialism is a fraud, a phantom. Compare yesterday with today's anarchist destroying our government to make way for a type of dictatorial control. What plausible reason would cause a sane person to tire of freedom?

On another day, we visited the Certosa di Pavia, a large monastery and complex in Lombardy, Northern Italy, near the province of Pavia. Certosa is the Italian name for a house of the cloistered monastic order founded by Saint Bruno in 1044. The monastery built in 1396 was one of the largest in Italy. Today, only scattered parts remain but still beautiful structures to observe. The Certosa is renowned for the exuberance of its architecture in both the Gothic and Renaissance styles and for its collection of artworks. The history of the Certosa is very interesting and worth a study.

We had lunch at Pavia in a delightful little outdoor garden restaurant. Huge hydrangeas, pastel-colored blossoms and deep-green leaves, dangled next to our table in a room of cool-mint green. The ambience simply took my breath away. Peaceful and very, very beautiful, almost like a fairyland. This was a lovely day. I do intend to one day capture this feeling in oil.

Tuscany

While touring Tuscany, we spent several days and nights in the medieval hill town of San Gimignano, a delightful experience I shall never forget. The ancient town had a skyline of towers encircled with thirteenth-century walls. The La Cisterna Hotel, still under construction, and a bakery were the only businesses open. The population was sparse. After many lost years, the town had not yet fully recovered from WWII.

Our accommodations were outstanding, the food and wine splendid. We never failed to overindulge every evening. The wine was awesome, especially the white. We took several cases back to Milano. Tuscany is wine country, where miles of vineyards spread across rolling hills emanating beauty, peace, and tranquility under cloudless skies. The cool nights were breathtakingly beautiful. As far as the eye could see, a blanket of stars shimmered across clear navy-blue skies. Tuscan skies radiate color like no other. After dark, we could see lights glowing from distant hill towns checkered across the landscape, each one a little spot of light luminous in the night. Tranquil.

As Patricia was fluent in Italian, we had no problem conversing with the people. Each day was a new and exciting adventure through the wine country's beautiful vineyards. Attempting to capture the emotion, the atmosphere in a painting of a tranquil farmhouse surrounded by vineyards was a fun challenge. Tuscany's tranquil ambiance reaches to the heavens. The painting hangs above my sofa.

During WWII, an assortment of people left the cities and found safety behind the walls of San Gimignano. During the war, German soldiers periodically appeared, flexing their muscles, annoying the people and always in search of Jews for the Gestapo to slaughter. There were Jews in San Gimignano safely hidden away from prying German eyes seeking their demise. Praise God, undiscovered.

All my life, certain sounds, smells, and places aroused a keen sense of having been there. San Gimignano is one of those places. There is a wonderful San Gimignano movie with an all-star cast that I own and periodically enjoy watching. *Tea With Mussolini.* Yes, I could live in Italy's hill country.

Who lived in Italy before the Romans? The Etruscans, in what is now known as Tuscany. They dominated Italy's trade with other cultures like Greece and the Middle East. They traded iron tools, weapons, Etruscan pottery, gold, and silver across the Alps to other nations, and they also imported slaves. You got that, slaves. Tuscany was annexed by Rome in 352 BC.

Florence came to overshadow and conquer all other cities in the region. Florence was ruled by an oligarchy of wealthy aristocrats, among whom the Medici family became dominant in the fifteenth century. Because of its dominance in literature, the Florentine language of the Italian region is the language of Italy today. Powers rise and fall; nothing new under the sun.

Florence

Florence is home to masterpieces of Renaissance art and architecture. The duomo is a cathedral with a terracotta-tiled dome and a bell tower by Giotto. A visit through Florence would not be complete without seeing Michelangelo's magnificent *David*, a masterpiece of Renaissance sculpture created in beautiful white marble between 1501 and 1504. It was so white it seemed to glisten under the dome's light. The Galleria dell'Accademia houses the seventeen-foot figure of the biblical David standing on a five-foot platform under a glass top dome. Thankfully,

I didn't know what to expect because as we approached the statue, I suddenly couldn't breathe, and tears blurred my eyesight. Can still close my eyes today and see David in all his glory, under a dome of natural light. I'm grateful to Patricia for affording me the luxury of seeing so many artistic masterpieces throughout Europe I had only seen in books.

CHAPTER 12

Missions

Before continuing our journey through history, my personal experience on the mission field will open your eyes, as it did mine, to the pure evils of poverty in third world countries. The desire to devote more time serving the Lord began to play heavy on my mind. Several years ago, living in Dallas, Texas, I attended a wonderful church active in evangelism training. We were scheduled for the South Pacific but had to stand down as unrest was rampant in the area. I was disappointed as we would have visited the Island of Bali. After taking the course, I joined a mission trip to Kazakhstan, an oil-rich communist country that borders southern Russia. We landed at Almaty, the south-eastern part of the country near the Chinese border. The population is about 2.7 million. This is where our troops land then deploy to service in various other locations.

Here are some interesting tidbits to share. The ancestor of the domestic apple is the *Malus sieversii*, which grow wild on the Tian Shan mountains. Scientists believe the Tian Shan apple seeds were first transported by birds and bears long before humans ever cultivated them. Almaty and surrounding lands are officially recognized as the Land of Wonders. According to the 2009 national census, 26 percent of the population are Christian, the rest either Islam or atheist. As Christians, we were not really welcome there. I registered as an artist and photographer.

Almaty is one of the ancient sites on the great Silk Road from China to Europe. The Silk Road was an ancient network of trade routes established during the Han Dynasty of China, linking the regions of the ancient world in commerce between 130 BCE to 1453. I loved being in the midst of ancient history, my mind whirling like a pin wheel. The Silk Road was shut down by the FBI and Europe on November 6, 2014. The Silk Road was an online black market and the world's first modern darknet market, best known as a platform for selling illegal drugs. Evil entities will never cease leaving behind death and destruction in their quest for riches. To the evil mind, preserving history is limited to fools. I am a fool.

In 1717, three thousand Russian slaves, men, women, and children were sold in Khiva by Kazakh and Kyrgyz tribesmen. In the period between 1764 and 1803, twenty Russian caravans were attacked and plundered. This is the story of two homeless sisters after the death of their father. The sisters traveled two thousand miles from their Kazakhstan home to Moscow, hoping for jobs in a grocery shop. They ended up enslaved by the shop owners. They fell prey to slave trade, estimated by the United Nations to affect forty million people globally, trapped in forced labor and forced marriage. The sisters escaped and are slowly rebuilding their lives. They are part of a lawsuit in the European Court of Human Rights; after all, legal routes in Russia and Kazakhstan failed to punish their former employers for enslaving and torturing them. The government of Kazakhstan has been fighting slavery since 2009 when instances of forced labor and bonded labor were found in the country's tobacco plantations. This world is Satan's domain. Will people ever wake up?

Kazakhstan's president Nursultan Nazarbayev, a member of the communist hierarchy, was given the position for life years ago. Other Russian intellectuals were exiled to the region. He supported Boris Yeltsin against the attempted coup in August 1991 by the Soviet extremist. The Soviet

Union fell apart after the coup failed. Nazarbayev went to great lengths to maintain close economic ties toward Russia by introducing Kazakhstan into the Commonwealth of Independent States.

On January 10, 1999, the date of a new election, Nazarbayev was barred from running in the election. Apparently, cheating means nothing to the American democratic elections either. Notice how evil power operates. A new law had recently passed, prohibiting anyone convicted of a crime from running in the election. The opponent, Kazhegeldin, was recently convicted of participating in an unsanctioned election rally, thereby became ineligible. Any old excuse will do. Cheating in elections means absolutely nothing to the Communist Party. It never has and never will. You only know what you know.

Nazarbayev ruled as a dictator, accused of human rights abuse by several human rights organizations. In 2002 it was reported that Nazarbayev had in the mid-1990 secretly stashed away $1 billion of state oil revenue in Swiss banks accounts. He suppressed dissent and continued to preside over an authoritarian regime until 2019.

Power always has a way of escape to deny or justify abuse of any kind brought to light by righteous people or competing evil organizations. Do you really want socialism in this country? Disgustingly prevalent today in America's liberal press and media. The little people, the populist at large have no idea the dangers that will befall them once our constitution has vanished. America's freedoms are hanging by a thread this very moment. The goons behind the scenes secretly pulling the strings and will eventually cut our thread of safety. Believe it!

On March 19, 2019, Nursultan Nazarbayev unexpectedly resigned after serving for thirty years. Kassym-Jomart, the incumbent president, had assumed the presidency three months before the elections following Nazarbayev's resignation. Tokayev was reelected with 71 percent of the vote. Any new lying voice will do.

There is valid evidence of Hunter Biden's connection to corrupt government officials in the new regime. Fox News had Hunter Biden's ex-business partner on air for an hour giving his personal testimony on the Biden connection to the China and Kazakhstan governments. Of course, the liberal news avoided this mind-opening information and continue in complete denial. It is a mystery to me how intelligent people ignorantly swallow propaganda, never concerned that truth is out there to embrace. "Blind eyes will be opened" (Isaiah 35:5).

Almaty, the capital of Kazakhstan, served as the Kazakh Soviet Socialist Republic from 1929 to 1997, population two million-plus, the country's largest city. In 1997, the government relocated the capital to Akmola (renamed Astana 1998) in the north of the country, on the banks of the Ishim River. The capital city was renamed Nur-Sultan after the former president.

This oil-rich country attracts all sorts of money hungry men. Through oil money and foreign investments, Almaty now has eight-star high-rise hotels, casinos, Turkish fast food, and American steak houses. Capitalism at all levels has been a free-for-all, with a few people grabbing all of the power regardless of who suffers. Namely, the Bidens vie for their piece of the action. If not jailed, Hunter Biden has more than his foot in that door. Of course, a full-force propaganda machine will soon appear, defending Hunter Biden. Surely Hunter's halo gives him a headache. The culture between the haves and have-nots was peaceful until recently, when the evil despots arrived to rob them blind. Now terrorism has shown its ugly face. Very interesting. Is communism still fighting capitalism? You bet it is! What a mixed-up world we live in.

This mission trip opened my eyes even more to the evils of socialism. Never forget, socialism is the decisive step to communism. Overall, Almaty was a beautiful city, not so nice in our location. One thing that blew my mind was garbage piled up and down our street and scattered everywhere throughout the city. What an eyesore. The reason for the constant clutter was a throwback from the hardline communist days when throwing something down gave someone else a job picking it up. Is this considered logic? Just more absurdity! Any service people, restaurants etc., were in no hurry to assist you because their salaries did not change if they rushed or stood still. Too much lunacy! This was also the case when I spent time in Russia. I don't see our nation of pampered individuals eager to fall into that fray, and that includes all the oblivious young rich kids out protesting the hand that feeds them.

We met unbelievers those few weeks. Sergia, a young Korean man with East-West Ministries, lived in Almaty; he was our guide. Sergia was born and raised in Almaty. He had the clever idea to rent an old empty, run-down building then put a large billboard out front saying, "Free English lessons." People showed up. After class, we had refreshments, gave our testimonies, visited, and answered questions about our country and sometimes about Christianity.

One weekend, we had a class picnic besides roaring waters racing through the outer foothills of the Tyan Shan mountains, about ten miles from the Chinese border. Uniquely beautiful! I found a tranquil spot to put my blanket where the mesmerizing sounds of water crashing over massive boulders topped off a perfect day. While sitting on my blanket, two attractive young girls approached me. They were college age, inquisitive, and filled with questions about Christianity. Very pleasant young ladies. One of the girls, a very beautiful tall brunette, the other a pretty cotton top with short straight white hair, fair skin, and lovely light blue eyes.

After answering a few key questions, the little blond showed a real interest in Christianity. Nothing more than curiosity, but a door was opened. The other girl said her Muslim family would not approve. It was apparent she came from a wealthy family. I commended her for honoring her parents but said not to forget that in time, her search for truth will lead her to make her own decisions about many things. She listened! In all, it was a lovely day, good company, and seeds of truth were planted.

On another day, a young girl and her mother from Uzbekistan risked their lives slipping across the border to spend the day fellowshipping with us. They secretly connected with East-West Ministries. Precious people.

Their journey was dangerous as Christians face death in Uzbekistan. Their ministry was all underground.

Their story, their plight, touched the depths of my soul as a witness to Almighty God, who inspires our every move and served to remind me, we are not given a spirit of fear. Loving, touching, and praying with these wonderful ladies caused me to rethink my lifetime of freedoms, taken for granted, wasting time on nothing. We really have no complaints. These brave ladies never draw a free breath because they are Christians in a closed, evil Islamic world. Their life's existence—their courage, bravery, and strength—depended solely upon faithfully trusting the Lord. These ladies were prepared to die for their faith.

Just recalling their story still brings tears to my eyes today. My heart is filled with joy for their outstanding faith and witness. One day soon, we may also lose our freedoms; they are hanging by a thread now. Just because I point these things out doesn't mean I am fearful of everything, I am not. Bring it on!

A lovely young Kazakh girl invited us for lunch at the home of her parents. Although her parents were Muslim, they never interfered with her choice of Christianity. They lived in a very small village in a modest small house. We sat down, said grace. I wasn't quite sure what I was looking at on my plate. Although the food was tasteless, I managed to eat. However, there was a suspicious-looking little round piece of meat glaring at me from my empty plate. Nothing to do but hold my breath and go for it. Only the tiniest bite confirmed my suspicions; it was no doubt horse meat. It may have been delicious, but I'll never know, and you may tell the horse I said so.

The Tian Shan, also Tengri too (meaning, celestial mountains), is a large system of mountain ranges located in Central Asia. The highest peak is Jengish Chokusu at 24,406 feet high; its lowest point is below sea level. Stretching 1,500 miles from west-southwest to east north-northeast, it straddles the border between China and Kyrgyzstan. It was a blessing to have experienced the people and nature's incredible beauty in this ancient part of the world.

CHAPTER 13

Burkina Faso, Africa

This was another occasion when I joined a mission group for Burkina Faso, West Africa, the third poorest country in the world, the town of Ouagadougou. Quagga (Wagga) lacked the beauty and graceful landscapes of Kazakhstan, yet blessings abounded. Wagga was also a Muslim terrorist training ground. Quite another eye-opening experience I shall never forget. We were on constant alert for terrorist activity.

The bush people live in a compound of grass huts with little surrounding walls as protection from wild animals. The huts were for sleeping, wall-to-wall bed only. The women always had a little fire burning outside with a pot for cooking. Throughout the countryside, women were squatting on the ground, tending their cook pots. We counted our blessings every day. We observed that the women did all the work. Never once catching the men doing anything constructive, mostly sitting around, talking, or sleeping.

The life span of these people is around fifty to sixty years or less. We met once in the local church, giving our testimonies but mostly met in the bush. My first time to stand behind a pulpit. There is no denying I was nervous.

Eddie was my roommate. We quickly bonded as Eddie was a friend of my daughter Patricia. When Eddie told me about her upcoming trip to Africa, I immediately wanted to join her. So off we went to Ouagadougou. Our so-called hotel room was old with exceptionally small rooms, barely room for two small single cots, luggage and two people. Americans have walk-in closets larger that these little cubicles. The toilet and lavatory were in a tiny closet, no room to turn around. Forget a bath! The showerhead was hanging slightly above the commode. Thank God we had immunizations before leaving home.

Our first African meal was in the hotel. Thinking chicken was the safest bet, I foolishly ordered chicken. This scrawny little bird wasn't boneless; it was meatless. At that moment I suddenly recalled flocks of scrawny, almost featherless chickens running around outside the hotel. There is exactly where they chased my supper down. After that ordeal, I chose to eat in a restaurant only once. Then things deteriorated. Ordered soup thinking that was a safe bet. Not to be! There was no liquid, only dried-up little somethings in the bottom of a metal bowl. This award-winning presentation was deliberate as my party had all ordered full meals. The waiter could drop dead waiting on me to complain. I never opened my mouth nor changed my facial expressions. After this washout, I decided the best thing was to eat a huge breakfast of scrambled eggs, lots of mangos, coffee, and fill up on bread. That plan worked out very well.

Every morning, just outside the hotel entrance, we very cautiously walked past two huge Brahman bulls tethered in mud and debris. Wasn't a friendly odor either. After a long van ride through the bush, the villagers were eagerly awaiting our arrival. We met under the canopy of the largest tree I have ever seen. The men stood on one side, women on the other, and the children sitting below us in the front. We were cautioned to speak clearly, slowly, and to say as few words as possible. By the time English translated into French and then into the local dialect, there was no telling what reached ears at the end of the line. All the children were attentive and exceptionally well behaved. Never saw better.

One young man caught my eye; he was intently hanging on every word spoken. Blessed to capture this moment
in a wonderful oil painting of this young man. He had on a
red sleeveless top with straps held together with huge safety
pins, obviously his mother's old blouse. Then a painting of
all the children sitting quietly on a bench, awaiting further
instructions. Precious, obedient children. Africa provided
enough heartwarming moments to inspire my "art spirit"
for years to come. These people, despite their abject poverty are kind, loving, and grateful for any little crumb of
kindness.

Unfortunately, Burkina Faso is no longer a safe place
for Christians. As a terrorist training ground, Burkina Faso
stays under alert. Today, it's no longer just a threat but open
for business. Let us all take a page from their playbook and
earnestly pray for the safety of these people. Pray for the
local Christians who do live in unrest. Their faith is the

only thing that sustains them. Faith is all any of us really need.

A couple of young black Christian men invited us to lunch one day. Since eating had been such an ordeal, I shuddered at the thought of another dreadful experience. In my heart, I knew I had to be gracious this time and trust in the Lord to see me through lunch. I was prepared to be outside squatting on the ground, eating no telling what. Well, praise God lunch was in a little one-room house in the middle of nowhere with a little front porch, like a very large playhouse. I gave a sigh of relief at the sight of a real house of sorts.

As we got out of the van, our host was standing in their aprons, grinning from ear to ear, obviously incredibly proud and happy to see us—and more than that, wanting to please us. On the porch were two cook pots, one with disinfection for hands, the other with water for rinsing. Perfect combination for the bush.

The little room was wall to wall with a large sofa and three large chairs and a low table in between. There was one small window high up that gave very little light. No light, no legroom. In the middle sitting on the low table was a large platter of rice mixed with something. Nestled atop the bed of rice was an ugly huge fish head on one end and the large tail sitting erect on the other end. These guys were obviously proud of their presentation. So I made a point to notice their handiwork. Knowing I had to trust and obey no matter what, we gathered around the little table for prayer. Lunch could no longer be avoided. Well friends, I went back for seconds. The food was absolutely delicious, well-seasoned and tasted much like my South Louisiana jambalaya. Our host was studying our faces the entire time, and when I took seconds, I thought they surely would break into dance at any moment.

Before leaving, we took each one by the hand, hugged them, blessed them, and thanked them for a wonderful meal. After experiencing an African gourmet lunch in the middle of the bush, we felt very privileged and blessed. No doubt, the bush is not a place for the finicky nor the pessimist.

No matter where or what we did, I was always treated with the utmost respect; the people rarely, if ever, encountered anyone age seventy-four. Testimony about the tragic life of my youngest son had touched the hearts of every mother there. On another day headed for the bush, I decided to wear my new very red dress covered with white leaves that I purchased at the artisan market in town. Our van came to a stop at the village. As we got out, the people always gathered around us. As I hopped off the van and started to walk, the crowd began to gather on either side of me. Saying to myself, "This stupid red dress is too much."

Having no idea what was happening, I just kept on walking until the people began to close in, forming a circle around me. To my shame I was a little frightened. Then a little four-foot-tall woman stood before me; her shriveled face came to life with the broadest grin you can ever imagine. She then squatted down, brushed the dust from my feet with a little homemade straw broom, then bent down and kissed the top of my feet. I was speechless!

As that precious, frail little lady stood before me, I saw a genuine love and respect alive in her eyes never seen before or since. With tears streaming down my face, I laid hands on her, blessing her in the name of Jesus. She looked to be the eldest member, chosen to bless and honor me in the name of Jesus. This blessing was mine to cherish forever. Obviously planned by the entire village to show respect and empathy for the tragic loss of my son. If that wasn't a humbling experience, I don't know what is. God truly had a purpose for this in my life at that time. And still holds true today. It's hard to hold back tears when I think of the humbling experience that transpired that day in the African Bush. Lessons of affirmation top the list. Knowing for sure my heavenly Father was in the midst of these godly people and on top of my life big time.

The purpose for going to Africa was to serve God and bless the people. Well, God blessed me with a power beyond anything I have ever known, and it remains firmly planted today. God had other plans in mind for me besides blessing local Christians. Humility reached the depths of my prideful soul. "Let go and let God" is an amazing truth I came to fully understand for the first time in my Christian walk. "Wisdom's instruction is to fear the Lord, and humility precedes honor" (Proverbs 15:33).

On another day trip, we visited a little one-room school located out in the middle of nowhere. The students were teenagers. Never have I seen teenage children so attentive and appreciative. They clung to our every word. I spoke about art and the art spirit, assuring them that our talents are a gift from God. Thankfully, I welcomed a captive audience. These innocent faces inspired my presentation. Wished it possible to take them home with me and fix things, buy the girls a pretty dress. As we were leaving, our van was surrounded with happy faces and hands reaching through the windows seeming to cling to the moment. Another wonderful humbling experience. Left there with a big lump in my throat.

We also visited an orphanage housed in an old two-story building left to self-destruct. The place was overwhelmed with unwanted babies. Bless the young women lovingly caring for these children. Lots of mouths to feed, formula to make, and diapers galore. Heartbreaking reality has a way of invoking awareness, at the same time hopelessness, void of resolution. A painful heart is threatening; I've been there. This was one of those times and another lesson for me. In retrospect, God's voice was loud and clear: serve!

Interfaith relations between the Muslims and Christians in Burkina Faso have historically been good. Since 2015, there have been increasing attacks on Christians by Salafi jihadists in Burkina Faso, which have escalated rapidly since 2017. This comes as no surprise since this area has been and is now a terrorist training ground. In 2019, Islamist gunmen killed five Protestant worshipers and their pastor as they were leaving church in the village of Silgadiji near Mali. In May 2019, four Catholics were killed by Islamists. In August 2019, four more Christians were executed by Muslims for wearing crucifixes. On December 1, 2019, fourteen churchgoers were killed in an attack when suspected Islamist gunmen opened fire on the church during services. In February 2020, a Protestant church was attacked during services, killing twenty-four.

We are only seeing the beginning; this evil will eventually reach America if our people and leaders do not soon wake up. Believe it! Here are sixty-four human beings slaughtered in cold blood only because they chose to freely worship the God of their choice. This evil is simply unfathomable. Yet there is nothing new under the sun. Would these murdered "black Christians lives" matter at all to the idiots running though our streets, destroying property and lives? Of course not! They are unaware. They have been spoon-fed hate and fear from the cradle. Now they are fed American dollars as well. As Marxists, they have no god, only the little human gods cleverly leading them around by the nose.

Fear in Africa is the politician and the witch doctor's strongest weapon as a means to control a society. From inception, the African people were overburdened with fear and superstitions. The witch doctor is very active in Burkina Faso. He is in the business of peddling fear, bones, and trinkets to ward off evil spirts or casting evil spells. Then for a price, the witch doctor was your man to cancel the curse. This is the closest I've ever visually been near Satan's domain and within earshot of his drums. He lived near the Ghana border a couple of miles from our little village. The old fool absolutely loathed our presence in his territory. Quite sure the little worm had several dozen curses working overtime and all to no avail. Covered with prayer each day against the sounds of beating drums as the old witch doctor practiced his voodoo. We were never once fearful of anything. We also slept very well in our little cubbyhole each night. There was no doubt in my mind that the Lord sent me to Africa, and He was faithfully watching over us.

"The only thing to fear is fear itself." President Franklin Roosevelt, in his inaugural address at the depths of the Great Depression.

"Fear not because I am with you; be not dismayed, for I am your God; I will strengthen you, I will help you, I will uphold you with my righteous right hand" (Isaiah 41:10). Now that's power I can and do receive.

Each day, a young woman brought to our meetings sat motionlessness on the ground, chained to a tree, her gray eyes void of life. We prayed over her daily with no response. We knew the people were hoping for a miracle, yet we failed to see one. Who knows, the power of God may heal her at any time after we leave Africa.

On a personal note, for a long time after returning home, visual images of the girl periodically pop into my mind. Anytime I'm praying about this lost young woman in Africa spending her life in chains, a visual image of her smiling face pops into my mind every time, seeing that she is with the Lord. If the witch doctor put that curse on her, she is now free from his curse. Evil carries a big ugly stick, but God carries a bigger one and a much larger heart.

This is the same evil destroyer deceiving the BLM and Antifa gangs into believing they are superhuman, judge, and jury. Evil has many faces and many ideologies to cypher. These uninformed rioters are well versed in Marxist doctrine, ignorant of its lies and dangers. Marxists will lie about anything any time if it serves the purpose. They are anti-God, satanic forces working throughout the universe. Wish they were chained under a tree with a blank stare on their faces.

The Bible clearly says this world is temporarily Satan's domain. Satan was defeated at the cross. Until Jesus returns to rule, Christians have the Holy Spirit within us to contend with the devil's schemes. Although I know without a doubt that justice is coming, this world will often challenge my patience. Never my faith. Check out this truth for yourself before you deny the facts. Remember, you only know what we know.

All lives matter because we are created in the image of God, our Creator. Denying this gives rise to "survival of the fittest," which deems human life of no noteworthy value. British philosopher Herbert Spencer first coined the phrase. Then Darwin used Spencer's new phrase as a synonym for "natural selection" in the fifth edition of *On the Origin of Species*, published in 1869. Biblical truth has not changed in over four thousand recorded years of human history. People consistently look for answers in all the wrong place for all the wrong reasons, so they will naturally cling to whatever tickles the fancy. In time, truth has become fables. Denying creation will never invalidate God's truth. Rest assured we did not evolve from yuck. Men, in their quest to disprove the Bible, have ascertained the truth of God's Word. You only know what you know. Humankind limits himself when depending solely upon his own understanding or erroneous teaching that will lead us in the wrong direction every time. People will inevitably miss the mark.

There is a biblical account of a woman over two thousand years ago accused of adultery by the scribes and the Pharisees. The Law of Moses commands them to stone such women. This is when Jesus said, "Let he who is free of sin cast the first stone at her" (John 8:7). No one fit those shoes; they all walked away. Jesus said to the woman, "Go and sin no more." Jesus of the New Testament is all about love, kindness, and forgiveness. Jesus offers us true freedom. How can anyone in their right mind ignore these beautiful, comforting truths? Why choose to live in a state of complacency or a confused state of mayhem and murder? Don't be an unsuspecting victim sucked into violent propaganda. It amazes me how relatively intelligent human beings can spend a lifetime wallowing in self-pity while drowning in a bloodbath of deceitful lies. Get a grip! Jesus Christ *liberated* women.

Think about it: no one is free of sin; no one is perfect. Change the name a million times, sin called by any other name is still sin. We just need to stop grazing in the devil's pasture. Disbelief will never invalidate the truth. Many people have no understanding of what constitutes sin or that sin even exists. Wake up! Evil is all around us. African people experience the reality of fear daily because fear is ingrained from birth. What a horrible existence. God has hardwired humankind with an innate awareness of right and wrong. Listen to your inner voice! We are without excuse. Menacing evil will gladly keep your mind in a choke hold. These lost fools tearing up our cities have no concept of truth because their hearts have been hardened, some from drugs. It's much more than just dulling the senses.

I really hesitate to put a damper on our wonderful journey to Burkina Faso, but the point must be made that evil men with evil intentions are everywhere. It turned out that Ram Zongo, our supposedly African Christian leader, embezzled every cent he could from East-West Ministries located in Dallas, Texas. He sent fake photographs of completed work to the Dallas ministry. The plan was to send him $2,000 from proceeds of my art show to dig a much-needed well. After I was informed of the truth, I directed $1,500 for the well through another source. It is difficult to always know who is for real and who isn't, and the problem is not limited to just third world countries.

We saw firsthand what real poverty looks like. We can hate the sin and love the person. Truthfully, I have zero compassion for all the privileged white college kids out beating the bushes alongside the Marxist BLM terrorists, yet I do pray for them. The entire absurd group of misfits should be forced to live as a native in the African Bush for a month or two, squatting on the ground to eat and defecate. People burdened with low self-esteem are desperately in need of recognition and to belong. Africa might persuade these lost souls they are not so bad off after all. It is not the privileged youth or the wealthy privileged adults jetting across the globe who experience the poverty-stricken people. If they do, it is most certainly from a safe distance. The have-nots truly transcend the haves worldwide.

CHAPTER 14

Moral Revulsion

Evil spins the very best lies. Our universities are so liberal that the students have no idea of what truth is or if truth ever existed. Truth as objective truth is no longer taught our youth. It's called "truth decay." Students say there's no such thing as truth. "Truth is a tool of White Supremacy." Absurdities! Students at Pomona College are demanding their president take disciplinary action against a student-journalist writing for *The Claremont Independent*, a conservative paper. In view of these misguided students, search for truth is little more than an attempt to silence marginalized people. If truth does not exist, then neither does the word *fact* or *factual* or its synonyms *accurate, authentic, historical* to name a few. If *truth* doesn't exist, then pray tell, why is truth so dangerous and feared? First, history must be revised or destroyed, promoting lies in order to alter a society's beliefs and its language. God help us once my generation dies along with the truth. And He will!

On a scale of one to ten, liberal professors are ten to one conservative. What young mind can survive these odds day after day? Parents had better wake up or sacrifice their children to another overpowering evil force. If you don't reach them, someone else will.

Antifa and BLM are Marxist terrorist organizations funded by evil men with plans to crush our country and our Constitution no matter the cost. They are slaves trained to incite violence and mayhem. Believing there is no such thing as good versus evil opens the door to chaotic disorders that will destroy a society, causing moral revulsion and suppressing society with abominable cruelty. George Soros funds both groups and also the four liberal news media along with other entities. Evil is an expert at sucking in the needy, the downtrodden, the ignorant, the greedy idle rich, and for what purpose? To turn their hearts into resentful, ravenous wolves in search of prey and to put fear in the hearts of the American people. Just spewing out lie after lie to a gullible people.

Communism and all dictators govern by fear. Suppose they don't know anything about that. Do you ever see people trying to break into communist countries? For what? American freedom is what people seek no matter the cost. The phrase "fear not" is found at least eighty times in the Bible. The enemy uses fear to decrease our hope and limit our victories. "Submit to God, resist the devil and he will flee from you" (James 4:7).

When people are totally wrapped up in self, they blindly lash out in search of any place to park their own deep-seated anger. These misguided people have total disregard for who or what falls in their path. When your whole existence is nothing more than a self-absorbed, self-deluding lie, it's difficult to overcome. Why not choose to live in third world countries, see how far your whining complaints will get you. Remember Tiananmen Square?

Why does it excite people to burn our cities, beat up and murder innocent citizens? It is futile to run around killing people because they disagree with you. You cannot destroy the entire world no matter who or what you think you are. In the meantime, you are destroying yourself. That's nuts! In this present world, people will never all fit under the same umbrella, nor do they desire to. Evil regimes have zero compassion for the sanctity of life, except, of course, for their own. There is nothing wrong with being wrong. When people refuse to see and admit they are wrong, pride is the culprit. A prideful attitude is wrong. The endgame of a lifetime of misdirected loyalties will always end in failure.

Envy is another sickness plaguing humanity. Envy and pride are rooted in sin. The haves and have-nots are an age-old dilemma vulnerable to evil intentions that lack sincerity or meaningful content. Don't envy anything, especially the rich man's delicacies. Often, when enslaved to money, a person will lose all sense of reality. You can't snuggle up with dollar bills! Wealth becomes the ruling factor; enough is never enough. Mankind's inevitable response to this statement is, "I would sure like to try."

Years ago, when the market failed, men were jumping out of skyscrapers. These were people whose self-worth was in the value of money. Many may have left families behind because they selfishly could not face failure. This is prideful. No one can foretell all their tomorrows. Tomorrow is another day. I would rather be poor and free than rich and miserable. God blesses many Christians with wealth, those who walk with Him and serve Him with their wealth. This may come as a surprise to you. King Solomon of the Bible is the wisest and richest man the world has ever known. King Solomon is an interesting study we could all learn from. King David, the boy giant killer, was his father. Check them out.

Americans are faced with another challenge that will not be resolved quickly. The crux of the matter is "the one-world government" falling rapidly into place. This is when the privileged ruling class will consider it their right to exploit the middle class and the underprivileged. When the smoke clears, you will not be happy perched atop a pile of rubble with no place to go. It is ridiculous to think the government can know what people need when they cannot know a person's history, nor do they care.

Our history is being systematically destroyed at warp speed. If you don't know what happened before, there is no evidence of truth or failure in our past, no past to dictate the future. How convenient. Our churches will eventually be gone, burned to the ground. This futile attempt is useless because our beliefs live deep within the heart and not in a church building. Are they stupid? When a holy God has allowed evil to run its course, God will set up His government on this earth. Evil is disassembling the police, leaving communities at the mercy of drugged-up goons. We live in an imperfect world among imperfect people. It's a stupid move. People and nations need protection. I believe anti-police rhetoric will backfire on the Democrats. Actually, I am sure of it. It's just simply too illogical. They assault our military, our language, our family structure, and even our statues. Obviously, Satan is in a panic; he knows the end is near. Listen up, little robots, this is not rocket science! As you will see and hopefully believe, America is rapidly echoing the voices of ancient history.

All I can do now at my age is share my thoughts, write about God's truths, and express my beliefs and my anger in words while I still have a voice. The Lord gives us our faith when we are born again. We must pray to receive revelation and wisdom. Acting upon the knowledge of God's Word activates our faith. We have the faith of Christ. (see Gal. 2:20).

I would much prefer to be on the front lines, fighting for our country's right to exist. People need to know and understand that our problems are not always caused by someone else. Humankind loves to place blame anywhere, on anyone other than on self. How very boring! Children learn the art of placing blame early in life. We are responsible for our own choices today, regardless of our yesterdays. Admit you're wrongs and get on with it. Made more than my share of both good and bad choices, and so have we all. Bad choices poison faster than rattlesnake venom racing through your veins. It's hard to kill bad choices in our own strength, if not impossible.

After wrestling with an aggressive spirit my entire life, I have finally learned lasting self-control comes from the Holy Spirit within me. This doesn't make me perfect, but I am at least aware of my shortcomings. This is the fastest road to anyone's recovery. Yes, recovery! We all have short-comings; we are overly sensitive, insensitive, angry, lying, pouting, sulking, whining, jealous, know-it-alls and more.

I believe all these shortcomings manifest as pride living in prideful people. Pride is sin because it is centered on self. I remember a jingle we sang at about age seven. Sticks and stones will break my bones, but words can never hurt me. Duh! Took these words literally throughout my life. Consequently, it took a lot to hurt my feelings. All Christians would do well to overcome these self-centered flaws in our character. Mother told me many times to "consider the source and ignore it," or "let that roll off you like water off a duck's back." Think about it: pretty sound advice. No one is perfect, so don't get your knickers in a wad. In the eyes of God, only the Christian's inner spirit is perfect through Jesus. Until we cease living in denial, anger, and anxiety, we will keep right on chiseling away at our minds, our bodies, and our overall health as well. I don't have time for it.

In this world of imperfect people there will always be those holding resentments toward us or vice versa. Get over it! They could be the needy ones. Who cares who is right or wrong! We can never change other people only change how we react toward them. Accept other people for who they are despite sometimes getting a belly full. We will sometimes inadvertently make enemies in this world because no one is perfect. All you disillusioned perfect people may not yet grasp the depths of this wisdom. Arguments are futile. Responsibility is to let go and let God. He manages challenges far better than I can. Now that God is in control, I'm close to half speed. Life without the Lord is like dangling on a bridge to nowhere. That was me! Stopped dangling a long time ago. Patience is a virtue, and it really does come with age. Impatience will cause wise people to make wrong choices. And so it did.

Impatience is like racing at misery full speed.
—Richelle E. Goodrich

CHAPTER 15

Islam

Islam's anger and resentment are not just now awakening from a deep sleep. No! The onset of Islam's resentment began long before the Islamic religion first came into existence. The Abrahamic religions are Judaism, Christianity, and Islam. Over four thousand years ago, Abraham's Egyptian concubine Hagar had a son, Ishmael. Abraham and Sarah ignored God's promise of a son as Sarah was past childbearing age. Sarah told Abraham to go into Hagar. Hagar gave birth to Ishmael. Sarah, Abraham's wife, was childless.

When Abraham was a hundred and Sarah was ninety, she gave birth to Isaac, the son God had promised years before. After a while, anger, resentment, and jealously overcame Sarah. When Ishmael was about seventeen, at Sarah's insistence, Abraham put Ishmael and his mother, Hager, out into the desert. While Hager sat crying, the Lord spoke to her, promising that Ishmael would be the father of many great nations. And so he was.

This account of history is worthy of studying. Once again, the Bible has the answers. Christianity, Judaism, and Islam worship the same God of Abraham. Only Christianity believes Jesus is the Son of God. Gaining an understanding of this ancient historic conflict between Ishmael and Isaac will shed much light on today's problems of hatred. More than a four-thousand-year-old vendetta is a little much.

Hatred coupled with vengeance is never the answer to anything; it's a death sentence. Vengeance is disgustingly prevalent today as Muslims are brutally murdering Christians in many parts of the world. Why? Because the Quran calls for Muslims to kill anyone who leaves or denies the Islamic faith (Surah 9:5). Islam is hell bent on world domination. It is possible America will be besieged by some type of evil force. Yet Islam claims to be a peaceful religion. Not true! This is just another face reflecting the same evils as the Inquisition. Today's powers that be will turn on Islam as soon as it serves their purpose. Evil, unprincipled men do not want any religion serving as the opium of the masses. Idiots! Don't they realize this is impossible? You only know what you know!

The Islamic religion came along six hundred plus years after Jesus Christ. Islam is like the new kid on the block fighting for position. Do they not know God has fulfilled His promise to Ishmael? The prophet Muhammad had revelations leading to the Islamic religion. Christianity has many prophets in the Old Testament predicting Jesus as

Savior and New Testament prophets and eyewitnesses to Christ. We also have a few modern-day prophets.

After fifty years of in-depth study, I know without doubt Jesus is the Christ. I do not go around killing people because they disagree with me. True Christianity is not a religion; it is a personal relationship with Jesus Christ. Religion has to do with *do*s and *don't*s. Jesus doesn't tell you not to do anything. He shows us what to do. He tells us what sin is and the result of sin. The choice is ours.

You can say Catholicism is a religion, an entity unto itself. There is a substantial difference in the holy Catholic church and the Roman Catholic Church. The word *catholic* came from the Greek adjective *katholikos*, meaning *universal*. God's universal church of Jesus Christ relates to all true Christian believers. The *Roman* Catholics observe many Old Testament laws and honor allegiance to the Pope along with Jesus. The Pope is not a holy man. He is just a man. And the one we have now is a communist. The Christian's allegiance is to Jesus Christ, the Son of God, and not the Pope, preacher, or church leader.

The Roman church has a very dark, dreadful past. The Roman church murdered many innocent people during the Inquisition and by the ungodly Crusades. Popes killed each other and their families, all for the papal throne of power and riches. This is not something I would ever put my faith in. Roman Catholic Church history is a disgrace to Christianity. In many ways, still is.

Vengeance is futile, like a dog running around in circles chasing his tail. Mother used to say, "What's sauce for the goose is sauce for the gander." I grew up hearing these silly simple words, never once connecting them to vengeance. Silly, but I do have a point. Sounds innocent enough, however, the words no doubt suggest vengeance: payback! No matter how subtle, in time, words can and will entice your senses. Our choice of words is crucial because words do have power no matter how innocent they sound. We don't always know our words are perceived in the way we intended, so think before you speak. A closed-minded individual will filter every word through the lens of his own mindset. Tragically, this has been the major culprit hindering mankind's mental and spiritual growth from the beginning of time. We are all guilty.

CHAPTER 16

Awakened

People of all ethnicities often cross my path. The other day, the TV repairman was here. Asked who he was voting for in this election. With a blank look on his face, he said, "I've never voted. Not even registered to vote." Trust me he left here with something solid to think about. Complacency is a travesty of youth, mostly among noncollege students.

On the other hand, college professors have pushed students toward accepting a systematic brainwashing program of anti-Americanism. This is Marxism indoctrinating our children at the earliest possible age. Marxism is a demanding situation. Do you see people trying to break into communist countries? No! The herd mentality is perpetual and especially dangerous among our youth who recklessly take our freedoms for granted. The college classroom is the liberals happy hunting ground.

All generations consistently search for something or someone different to tickle their ears. Opinions are a dime a dozen; pick one. A parent's teaching may or may not deserve rejection. Youth will cling to the hope that this new experience might have the answer until it falls short. Answers for what? Youth rarely knows the question, much less the answers. All of mankind has an innate need to belong, to connect. Youth's inevitable lack of judgment leaves them vulnerable to the latest fads.

As a parent, I'm ashamed to say I did not properly prioritize all vulnerabilities in raising my children. I only knew what I knew based on my own limited experiences. This is a universal problem. I just bravely barreled through life, experiencing people along with mountains of uncertainty. I suppose I expected my children to do the same. Not too bright on my part. At times in my life, I experienced terrifying moments, mostly of my own doing. Occasionally, we will all encounter trouble, and in my case, that was life swimming upstream. Singing alto in the church choir, young people on Wednesday nights and family gatherings were my only outings until age fourteen, when I met Al Babin, my first husband, who was Catholic. His family wanted me to have our marriage blessed and take *instructions* in Catholicism from a priest.

I reluctantly agreed. When the priest told me I would have to raise my children Catholic, I immediately got a burr in my tail. Then he proceeded to explain rhythm to me: how to know when a woman was fertile. Well, that did it; two visits and I was out of there. This was the onset of my adulthood and my journey without Jesus, or so I thought.

Despite ignoring the Lord, He was there every step of the way. I just didn't fully realize it at the time. Years later, my daughter Karen confronted my Christianity. Praise God she did. At that time, my life was in shambles. God knew it, and He sent Karen to wake me from a deep sleep. Then one day, unbeknownst to me, the Holy Spirit took over. When I got sick and tired of being sick and tired, I sought help through prayer in the only way I knew how, on my knees. My life had mostly been full of ups and downs. Praise God my parents instilled Jesus in me from birth. Praise God for sending me Karen.

Most of my life I had only called on the Lord when trouble was knocking at my door. I had no concept of walking *with* Jesus. Later on, I came to understand Jesus had never left me alone. By then, I really had a hunger for the Word. There was so much truth not yet clear to me. My family attended church and Sunday school every Sunday after we moved to Baton Rouge. I attended Young Peoples Bible Study on Wednesday nights, and these were my only outings other than family visits until I was about thirteen or fourteen. This blessed sheltered life was about to subside.

"Footprints in the Sand"

You walked with me
Footprints in the sand
And helped me understand
Where I'm going
You walked with me

When I was all alone
With so much unknown
Along the way
Then I heard You say
I promise you
I'm always there
When your heart is filled
With sorrow and despair
I'll carry you
When you need a friend
You'll find My footprints in the sand

Song by Leona Lewis (Jesus is that friend)

During dark moments, these beautiful, comforting words uplifted me many times. Regardless of how far I fell, I never once denied my Christianity, my nationalism, or my patriotism. Mother gave me a Bible in 1953 that I read periodically.

It was not until we moved from French Settlement to Baton Rouge that we attended church regularly for the first time. There was no protestant church in French Settlement. I really got into Bible study with my dad, although I didn't understand much, except the words of Jesus written in red letters.

Around ten or eleven, I decided to tackle Revelation and found myself constantly crashing in despair. Daddy tried to explain things the best he could, but he wasn't well versed on end times. I'm not sure Presbyterians adhere to Revelation. My Sunday school teacher couldn't answer my questions either. The extent of my understanding was that one day, we would face evil power ready to destroy our peace and security and that Jesus would come for us when we died. Liked the sound of that. I've never really completely given up. So today, I'm up to my eyeballs in the Word, soaking it up like a giant sponge. Jesus is my team captain, and I'm not budging.

The youth of my day loved singing the national anthem and "America the Beautiful," among others we never hear today. Of course not! They have been removed; don't favor Marxism. So how can we expect our children to embrace patriotism? Evil entities will use lack of patriotism as a dividing tool against our nation and its people. We only know what we know. I'm afraid today's knowledge is bent toward liberal lies. I venture to say, all knowledge.

My generation was a product of WWII; I saw Hitler's evil lies firsthand. I understand the Great Depression and the effect it had on our lives. From my youth, I knew firsthand the depths of third-world depravity and corruption. My young mind was never idle. Thankfully, my parents were there to fill in the blanks when they could. Everything in life is a lesson learned, and my yesterdays are mine.

CHAPTER 17

Recent Wars

As we explore recent and ancient history, we see there is "nothing new under the sun." The purpose is to address slavery from antiquity to the present and the slaughter of multimillions by power-hungry, evil forces attempt to eradicate all opposition. With little or no knowledge of ancient history, most people are oblivious to the world's powerful leaders' true participation in mass murder, mayhem, and slavery, all under one banner or another. Slavery is slavery by any other name and has existed from the beginning of humanity. Slavery is not limited to Black people only, but all ethnicities are victims of this appalling practice.

Today's power-hungry moguls will play the race card as long as it serves their purpose, then when no longer useful, we will throw black people and every other color into the bottomless pit of extinction. Hopefully, your eyes and minds will recognize the malice of these despicable people and their objective to control an unsuspecting society.

We are without excuse. Praise God there are many highly educated men and women of color who are conservative, God-fearing human beings who cling to, teach, and speak the truth wherever possible. The black race has many, many strong Bible believing Christians who voted conservative in this presidential election. The Democrats feared losing the black vote and one of the reasons they stooped to cheating.

John Kennedy of Louisiana, one of my favorites, said this in his slow, deliberate voice: "Jelly fish have survived for 650 million years without a brain, so there is still hope for the Democrats yet."

Korea

The Korean war, 1950–1953, took place during my generation. America's armed forces were once again sent to battle in foreign lands. For centuries, the North Korean peninsula was a closed society, ruled by generations of dynastic kingdoms. More recently, due to the governments erratic control of farming, a famine killed two million people in 1990. This evil took place only thirty-one years ago; think about that. The lives of the people meant nothing to the ruling class and still doesn't. Today, much of North Korea's income derives from illegal narcotics, selling weapons, and human trafficking. Despicable!

Twenty-nine years earlier, the war began when North Korean troops pushed into South Korea on June 25, 1950, and it lasted until 1953. There was a division following

Japan's 1945 colonial rule over Korea for thirty-five years. After the Japanese Empire was dismantled at the end of WWII, Korea fell victim to the Cold War. Korea was then divided into spheres of influence along the thirty-eighth parallel. The Americans controlled south of the line; the Russians installed a communist regime in the north, later ceding influence to China. China has had designs on world power for years. Looks like President Biden is on China's team hook, line, and sinker, as well as his son and brother. Only God knows what's in store for America.

North Korea, armed with Soviet tanks, crossed the thirty-eighth parallel after WWII and quickly ran over noncommunist South Korea. The US came to their aid as part of a "police action" run by a UN international peace-keeping force. Nothing changed in the country. The war did not lessen the era's cold war. The war had kept the south from destruction by the evil powers of communism. It is the Northern communist seeking control of the South.

Does anyone care that nearly five thousand lives were lost, about ten percent of the prewar civilian population, which was higher than WWII's and the Vietnam War? Forty thousand Americans died in action, and more than one hundred thousand were wounded. This is nothing short of insanity. Two absolutely opposing worldviews will rarely ever agree. One advocates freedom; the other abolishes freedoms. Who bears the brunt? The little man, certainly not the rich fat cats sitting atop the heap. All these lives were sacrificed for nothing other than evil bearing its fangs in the face of peace. In time, this will happen again.

It looks like the time may be now. There is nothing new under the sun.

Slavery in North Korea formally existed from antiquity up to the twentieth century. Slavery was very important in medieval Korea; it was a major institution. Slavery began to decline in the eighteenth century. Although illegal today, forms of illicit modern slavery such as human trafficking exist. In the North, slavery is still practiced today by the country's regime. An estimate of 10.4 percent of the North Korean population is effectively enslaved as of 2018. Communist North Korea has one of the longest unbroken chain of slavery of any society in history, spanning about two thousand years. North Korea ranked highest in the world today that has not explicitly criminalized any form of slavery.

There are one million people in modern slavery via forced labor. Much of this communist country's income derives from illegal narcotics and selling weapons to terrorists. Why aren't the rioters over there tearing up this evil country. Why? Because evil controls that country; why disturb evil? Think about it! You only know what you know.

Vietnam, 1954–1975

According to Wikipedia, the cause was a parallel increase in support to the north from both China and the Soviet Union. The US got involved once more for fear of communism taking control; 2.7 million served. The US was unable to defeat the Vietcong and at the same time met with opposition back home. Everyone has an opinion, but opinions are just that, *opinions*. Groups or organizations planted the seeds of dissension among our society. Many, many people were fools. Who has a crystal ball? I'm not naive enough to believe our self-centered populous produced that scenario all by itself. In the meantime, one in ten soldiers were killed, 304,000 wounded. Communist forces ended the war by seizing control of South Vietnam. This ended a century of French colonial rule in Indochina.

US soldiers were prisoners for years in the so-called "Hanoi Hilton." Men either bowed to their captors or took severe beatings. They endured years of brutality and harsh living conditions, kept in bare, dark, concrete cells with little ventilation and forbidden contact with each other. The "rope trick": binding hands and elbows behind the back with manacles, then using rope to rotate them upward until the shoulder and elbows popped out their sockets, and for what purpose other than deriving pleasure from inflicting pain on helpless men simply because they could. The prisoners may have been the only control these pathetic little guards ever experienced over anything. Total power is quite the trip, especially for insignificant, mundane little people. Man's inhumanity to man is beyond the pale of decency. Our streets seem to manifest much of this same mentality today.

The practice of slavery in Vietnam has persisted since the Hồng Bàng period, when the society divided into three classes consisting of kings, citizens, and slaves. A slave, the lowest class, served the aristocracy. During the Chinese domination period, Vietnamese girls were sold as sex slaves to the Chinese. Evil regimes never change, they just get greedier.

As Americans, we should be outraged because of this same evil behavior is practiced in our own country. Wake up, America! It may not personally touch your life yet, but America's innocent children, young girls and boys, are sold into sexual slavery. It doesn't matter how young the children are, sometime the younger, the better. This is sick! All you self-centered idiots want to throw my kind to the wolves because we are conservative. Many are Christians. Why not search out the pervert's sex trafficking our innocent children? It's doubtful very many Americans are aware that our country is number one in the world for X-rated movies and sex trafficking. This may not disturb you, but it makes me mad as hell. Turning a blind eye will bring more monstrous evil upon our country than you can ever imagine. I refuse to close my eyes to it!

Cambodia

The Khmer Rouge, 1975–1979, was a brutal regime that ruled Cambodia under the leadership of Marxist dictator Pol Pot. Pol Pot systematically hunted and killed intellectuals, religious leaders, and city residents. He attempted to create a Cambodian "master race" through social engineering that led ultimately to the deaths of more than two million people in the Southwest Asian country. Those killed were either executed as enemies of the regime or died from starvation, disease, or overwork.

Adolph Hitler, in his pursuit of a "master race," used the same tactics and worse, if possible. This period in history has come to be known as the Cambodian genocide. Who pays attention anymore? Wake up!

The Khmer Rouge came into power in the mid-1970s. The roots of their takeover can be traced back to the 1960s, when a communist insurgency first became active in Cambodia. Throughout the '60s, the Khmer Rouge operated as the armed wing of the Communist Party. The Khmer Rouge did not have popular support among the Cambodians and for good reason.

For no good reason, our nation of youthful idiots are falling prey to communism. Have they lost their minds? No, they are thoroughly brainwashed. In early 1900, the progressive John Dewey promoted communist ideas through massive indoctrination in our public schools. This is exactly what Adolph Hitler did in Germany. Why is America shocked that communist doctrine has taken over our educational system and about to destroy our democracy? We are too trusting and haven't paid attention, that's why. My father fought against Dewey's progressive curriculums forced into public schools.

Later in Cambodia, a 1970 military coup ousted the ruling monarch Prince Norodom Sihanouk; an alliance was formed with the prince. For the next five years, a civil war raged in Cambodia. Eventually, the Khmer Rouge seized control and, thus, ruled the country. To no surprise, power never restored to Prince Norodom, but instead, the prince was forced to live in exile. So much for trusting alliances with evil. Do we really want communism or any other entity that crushes our constitution, our freedoms, and control of our country? Think long and hard about this because our freedoms are in jeopardy at this very moment. You won't know what you have until it's gone.

Afghanistan

This was the longest war in American history. On October 7, 2001, United State Forces began strikes on Taliban's Al-Qaeda forces. November 13, 2001, the US-backed Northern Alliance forces entered Kabul as the Taliban withdrew and within a month had fled into Pakistan. The conflict went on and on.

The United States's invasion of Afghanistan started in response to devastating terrorist attacks on the World Trade Center, September 11, 2001. I remember well waking up to that nightmare. There had never been anything like that on American soil, thank God. Much like WWII, people began to volunteer for the armed forces. Young people who may have never given thought to patriotism, suddenly became aware of our vulnerability. In response, the United States sought to remove the Taliban from power. Taliban forces, along with members of Al-Qaeda terrorists, were the main suspects. The Afghanistan war killed more than 2,300 US service members and wounded more than twenty thousand, while more than one hundred thousand civilians are estimated to have died.

While under President Trump, in late February of 2021, the US and the Taliban signed an agreement that included, eventually, the complete withdrawal of US forces from Afghanistan. This undercuts diplomats who have said withdrawal will depend on the Taliban's commitment to its peace deal with the United States. This all remains to be seen. These people have no problem agreeing to anything, knowing very well that in time their agreements will not hold water. President Trump called US involvement in the Middle East "the single biggest mistake in the history of our country." PS: Now that Biden is in power, he withdrew from Afghanistan and it was a disaster. He foolishly reversed everything Trump put into place.

Modern-day slavery in Afghanistan echoes the same reprehensible practices of old. There is nothing new under the sun. Afghanistan is a horrible place to be as a woman or a defenseless, vulnerable child. Women and children are trafficked as sex slaves both in country and to other evil regimes. Some of these men are well-armed warlords.

There is an ancient Afghan custom called *bacha bazi* where prepubescent boys dressed as women perform seductive dances for the entertainment of a group of men. Sounds like a group of pedophiles to me. This is a deeply embedded tribal practice that leads to rampant sexual abuse.

According to an article by Emily Prey and Kinsay Spears on American military in Afghanistan, "Over the decades of the American Military presence, the US continuously turned a blind eye to the Afghan National Security Forces (ANSF) and Northern Alliances' insistence that the current iteration of "bacha bazi" is Afghan culture. The reality is these groups are embracing a historical practice in order to traffic and severely abuse vulnerable Afghan boys.

The US Department of Defense was aware, by 2000, of the relationships between men and boys on US military bases in Afghanistan. The US overlooked multiple instances of criminal and gross abuse of children and human rights violations."

Atrocities are the same no matter how many smiley faces you live with or just how content you might think you are. Your world can come crashing down in an hour. People will conform to group expectations out of the human need for social approval and belonging.

Time to Think

Twenty years later, the scars remain. The World Trade Center was attacked as part of a series of four coordinated terrorist attacks by the Islamic terrorist group Al-Qaeda in retaliation against the United States' support of Israel and America's continued presence in Saudi Arabia after the Gulf War and our intervention in the Middle East. During the attack, 2,977 people died, nineteen hijackers committed murder-suicide, and more than six thousand others were injured. The immediate deaths including 265 on the four planes, 2,606 in the World Trade Center and in surrounding area, and 125 in the Pentagon. Wars never cease.

Some say the Quran, Islam's revealed text, "promises terrorists seventy-two virgins in Paradise." This will never transpire, but terrorists have been brainwashed, and seventy-two virgins is a mind-blowing lie. How can anyone believe such nonsense? It appeals to the flesh, and the flesh is weak; apparently, weak-minded as well. The devil will promise you most anything. Satan was even egotistical enough to tempt Jesus.

Jesus had rebuffed two earlier temptations. Standing atop a majestic mountain, Satan said to Jesus, "I will give You all these kingdoms, if You will fall down and worship me" (Matthew 4:9). This scene confirms the argument for supremacy of spiritual over secular power. At that time, the world was Satan's domain to offer until Jesus's death on the cross.

America has been involved in thirty-seven wars or conflicts of some kind with millions of lives lost: twelve major wars. America has been at war 93 percent of the time—222 out of 239 years—since 1776. America has only been at peace for less than twenty years total since its birth. The Indians fought to protect their lands from the white man. We fight to protect America's homeland from foreign entities, maintain our peace, our rights, and our Constitution.

These threats not only come from within but from foreign entities seeking total power. In the process of seeking world domination, Islam is now stirring up religious wars with approval from their populous. At the same time, unsavory oligarchs are using Islam to help foster vicious agendas before eventually feeding Islam to the dogs. Battles from within are the most dangerous of all. It is doubtful our dumbed-down society on the wrong side of political freedom is even aware that our way of life is threatened. No, they just keep on keeping on, tromping down the same paths of self-centered oblivion. This will continue until the day someone pokes out their eyes or confiscates their money. Life is not all about *self.* Nefarious activity by politically organized crime syndicates have openly accelerated plans to destroy America. There are no longer any secrets. The raw truth is there for those willing to open their eyes.

You will see that slavery has been a major part of world history since the beginning of time. Evil men lord over the little man because they can or think they can. There was no reparation back then, and there will be none now. It is important to realize that slavery is no respecter of color, race, age, or sex. Throughout humanity, people of all colors and ethnicities are kidnapped, abused, and identities gone, sold into slavery by the millions.

White slavery has been around forever. This is when women are drugged, tricked, forced into prostitution, then typically taken to a foreign country for this purpose. The real purpose: to line the pockets of lazy-ass, power-crazy, sociopathic little perverts. A destroyed life at the mercy of evil people should never be ignored. Worst of all is the sex trafficking of innocent children. This is an alarming worldwide enterprise, well organized and managed by wealthy scumbags. Our United States tops the list for pornography. God will not ignore this, and I hope soon.

The Biden administration and his goons are handing out reparations like candy, even giving them to people incarcerated. What does a lifer need with money, money I could use. Guess my skin's the wrong color, a disgusting white republican. Just more insanity like opening up the prisons, our borders, and defunding the police.

There is another heinous form of worldwide traffickers. Ruthless traffickers controlling the global trade of fresh kidneys prey on the poor, the sick, and the young. The illegal trade of kidneys has resulted in more than ten thousand transplants a year or more than one every hour. This is horribly wrong. In poor countries, the donor sells his kidney, then is left to survive or die from all sorts of complications. And in many incidences, people are murdered for their kidneys. Of course, the kidney traffickers deserve to burn in hell for eternity, and trust me, they will. People are ignoring these unconscionable satanic movements racing across our universe with great speed.

On a more personal note, unbeknownst to us at the time, my three-year-old son was abused by a disgusting, evil pedophile. Our son could have been younger. No way to find out. Lindsey could never remember when it started because he was too young. We often talked about his abuse and his life. Sexual abuse left my son on a path of destruction finally taking his life. My beautiful six-foot-one son was dead at thirty-one; only the shell of a human being was left. Praise God he died in the comfort of my arms, knowing he was deeply loved, forgiven, and that God loved him even more. He had accepted Christ as his Savior weeks earlier. He understood we would meet again in eternity.

After watching him suffer his entire life, death was a blessing. There is no time line for grief; anger still tugs at my heartstrings after all these years. The Lord says I must forgive. This is very hard because at times, I do still hate for a little while. Lindsey was just one of millions of children set adrift, lost in the bondage of sin. The world looks the other way. Closing blind eyes to evil is a major blot on all societies. Call it like it is: sin! Who among you is willing to take a stand?

Does anyone care or is even aware that multimillions of innocent people of all ethnicities were slaughtered down through the centuries, their lives sacrificed by malevolent power-seeking men. Our educational system is sacrificing our children in the halls of learning. They are no longer taught ancient history. History is repeating itself, and therefore, it's necessary to obscure the past. To the liberal mindset, truth is relative. One only needs to look around to see what relevancy gets you. This is another big fat lie! Absolute truth is never open for debate or dispute. These numbskulls just simply annihilate all who disagree while removing the word *truth* from our language.

Is this not absurd? Don't laugh; it's happened before. Children who deny the existence of absolute truth have no place to firmly anchor beliefs reflected in life, "like a fish out of water." Where are the parents?

One truth especially threatening our children is that dangerous pedophiles are roaming around, waiting for an innocent child to devour. This is an absolute fact. It is purported that homosexuals have no use for pedophiles. This is understandable and I believe true. What came first, the chicken or the egg? When children are abused from birth till ages three or four, they are unaware that same sex is not a natural desire. No, they often accept homosexuality as a lifestyle choice. Once the die is cast, choice becomes a factor. A lie! There was a saying back in the '60s: "sex before eight, or it's too late." What does this mindset tell you?

We've certainly come a long way. Sexual diversion is now taught in our elementary schools. Absurdity! Sex education is, first, the parents responsibility. Parents have neglected this all-important development in a child's sense of morality, understanding of right and wrong. Dereliction of duty opens the door for satanic forces to move in and take over. God's Word teaches me to love the person and hate the sin. I have gay friends whom I am very fond of, some I have known for years as a part of my life. It is not my place to judge anyone, and I don't.

Some desperate people look to ancient cultures' practice of sexual diversion in an attempt to justify their own sexual bent. Someone actually related this to me. You know my flood gate flew open. Past sins in no way justify present-day choices. Pagan cultures willingly sacrificed their children on the fires of Baal, Ashtoreth, and Molech, evil pagan gods. Today, abortion mills and pills.

Should we start throwing our children in the fire now? The danger is, where do you stop? Infant children are used by some sexual perverts then left to die. Babies sell at a premium. Children are murdered alive in the abortion mills, their body parts sold. This too is an abomination! Actually, the COVID vaccine may contain cells from aborted babies. For now, this is denied. If this is true, then it would be better to die of COVID than put this vaccine in my body. With the Lord's guidance, I don't plan to leave any time soon.

After six pregnancies, I know of what I speak. Even science says embryonic development is the beginning of life. Our Creator God says life begins at conception. People are either ignorant of what God says, or they deny the truth. Abortion is without doubt cold-blooded murder. In *this sense*, animals are treated better that humans. There are animal rights organizations to protect them. *Egocentric* is another choice of words for the so-called desensitized mind. People who choose the desensitized, morally neutral mindset are living in denial. No matter how you think it, believe it, write it, hear it, or say it, there is no denying absolute truths. It will come back one day to bite you.

All histories ancient to the present, recorded for posterity, will soon be systematically destroyed. Why? Recorded history will expose the lies and misinformation raging across the world. In time, the anything-goes society will naturally self-destruct. Then what? Out of sight, out of mind! This only works on shallow, ignorant, unconcerned individuals who choose not to see past their nose. Parents, wake up! Personally, I have witnessed the truth of sexual abuse firsthand by innocent-looking people. These predators are found at homes, churches, schools, neighbors, playgrounds—anywhere vulnerable children trod.

CHAPTER 18

History's Bloody Past

Throughout history, evil empires have come and gone. Brutal and devastating tyrants controlled their kingdoms. They showed little compassion for their people or their enemies. Human suffering repressed civil liberties, and lack of compassion caused the deaths of millions of people. The purpose for recounting some of history's evil empires will hopefully shed light on the fact that history does indeed repeat itself. The revising of history is a futile attempt to paint evil in a more favorable light, hoping to disregard our history completely. Lies and more lies especially highlighting the history of slavery, sexual perversion, and the murder of millions at the hands of despotic rule.

I'm encouraging our citizens to open their eyes and realize we are being duped by ruthless men interested only in promoting their own personal agenda: *power!* If you only listen to lies, how will you ever know the truth? Intelligent people question. Will the liberal masses eventually dissipate into the waste dumps of society? *Yes!* Question that!

This list is only a partial of past evil empires.

- British Empire
- Imperialist Japan
- Russia
- Mongol Ottoman Empire
- Genghis Kahn
- Third Reich
- Belgium
- Soviet Union
- Māori

The brutal Māori tribe warriors in New Zealand were cannibals and slave traders. Once the Māori got hold of muskets, tribal warfare broke out, leaving eighteen thousand people slaughtered. The horrific bloodshed between the British and the Māori lasted until the Māori's defeat. Even the Māori savages owned slaves. A society absent of God left to their own reasoning can easily reach the depths of depravity. The pattern is the same.

Belgium

The Belgian colonial empire consisted of three African colonies in the Congo, the third largest colony in Africa. Considered the private property of King Leopold II, he became known as "the Butcher of the Congo" for murdering millions of natives by forcing them to work on his rubber plantations. Those who failed to meet the quotas were flogged, or their hands were cut off. I don't believe the majority of plantation owners in our country adhered to this brutal practice.

Yes, evil men did exist, and God's justice will have the final word. There is nothing new under the sun. Brutal evil spirits propelled evil men throughout the universe. Grasp this truth! They are still hanging around.

Japan

The Japanese Army was responsible for the deaths of millions of civilians and prisoners of war, up to fourteen million people in total. They experimented on, tortured, starved, and enslaved the people they conquered. In 1543, a large-scale slave trade develop in which the Portuguese purchased Japanese as slaves and sold them to various locations, including Portugal itself. The Japanese slaves are believed to be the first of their nation to end up in Europe.

The Portuguese purchased hundreds of Japanese slave girls to bring to Portugal for sexual purposes. These women were sold as concubines to Asian and African crew members serving on Portuguese ships along with their European counterparts. Listen to this! The Portuguese owned the Malay slaves, who in turn owned Japanese slaves. In 1595, Portugal passed a law banning the selling and buying of Chinese and Japanese slaves.

Karayuki-san, meaning "Ms. Agone Abroad," were Japanese women who traveled to or were trafficked to East and Southeast Asia, Siberia, and San Francisco in the second half of the nineteenth century and first half of the twentieth century to work as prostitutes, courtesans, and geisha. The "yellow slave trade" also involved other countries. Wake up! This is in our lifetime.

All this is to say that slavery is and was in no way limited to black people. Predominately, women are sold into sexual slavery and rarely, if ever, escape. Just relating all this garbage turns my stomach, especially the disgusting men who dominate the trade.

British Empire

Here are some of the atrocities that occurred under British control, oligarchs. There were so many, it would take volumes to disclose them all. They rounded up people into concentration camps during the Second Boer War. Starvation and disease killed over twenty-seven thousand South African Boers. The Boers were of Dutch, German, or Huguenot descent.

The crimes of Winston Churchill are a terrifying account of how colonial rule is directly exploitative. Churchill made matters worse by making known his contempt for India and its people. This led to millions starving to death. Very few in Britain know about the Bengal genocide and how he engineered four thousand people starving to death during the Bengal famine. "I hate Indians, they are a beastly people with a beastly religion" (Churchill).

The British army took millions of tons of rice to the Middle East. When the Indians asked for food, he said the famine "was their own fault, for breeding like rabbits." He also said on the Middle East and India, "I am strongly in favor of using poisoned gas against the uncivilized tribes." Churchill sounds much like Hitler. "We have always found the Irish a bit odd; they refuse to be English" (Churchill)

In the Kongo, at least 150,000 men, women, and children were forced into concentration camps. Churchill shut down all schools, branding them "breeding grounds for rebellion." Rape, castration, cigarettes, electric shock, and fire—all used by the British to torture the Kenyan people on Churchill's watch. Some call Churchill a genocidal maniac. Oligarchs ruled England.

At one time, the sun always set on English territories. At its height, the empire governed a fifth of the world's population and one quarter of the world's total land area. Proponents say the empire brought various economic developments to parts of the world. Once, when protesters defied the British government, they were blocked inside a walled garden and fired upon by Gurkha soldiers. Under orders, the soldiers kept firing until they ran out of ammunition, killing 379 and another one thousand injured—all within ten minutes. The Brigadier was later lauded a hero by the British public, who raised twenty-six thousand pounds for him as a thank you. Praising a mass murderer is disgusting beyond words. Churchill's evil deeds far surpass anything positive he may have done.

The Gurkhas are soldiers native to South Asia of Nepalese nationality recruited for the British Army, India, and Singapore, supposedly for peace keeping forces. Well, slaughtering people inside a walled garden is in no way peaceful. Then rewarding the perpetrator is beyond a civilized people. Can't wrap my head around it.

Borders drawn between India and the newly created state of Pakistan, split the subcontinent along religious lines, uprooting over ten million people. Forced to leave their homes, violence ruled the day. Estimates suggest up to one million people lost their lives in sectarian killing. Who caused it all? The English!

Due to famine, Churchill also ordered tons of wheat sent to Britain. Let the Indians starve. We are witnessing deliberate violent uprisings in America today. Never lose sight that an overall plan is behind all the violence. Look for oligarchs to mount our throne. Let the people starve.

Winston Leonard Spencer Churchill was born at Blenheim Palace in Oxfordshire on St. Andrews. This was the home of his grandfather, the seventh Duke of Marlborough. On his father's side, he was a child of the aristocracy; his father was the conservative politician Lord Randolph Henry Spencer-Churchill. His mother was the American-born beauty Jennie Jerome, daughter of a New York stockbroker, financier, and newspaper proprietor. They were a glamorous, high society couple but were distant parents. Distant parents always create a void in a child's life no matter who you are.

Mau Maus

An African secret society originating among the Kikuyu people of Kenya. In the 1950s, they used violence and terror to try and expel European settlers, ending British rule in Kenya. The British eventually subdued the Mau Maus, but Kenya gained independence in 1963. During the 1951 to 1960 uprising, British forces mistreated, raped and tortured them. Some estimate deaths at twenty thousand, others at one hundred thousand. Without doubt, the British empire is seriously guilty of major war crimes. Oligarchs rule Britain. Chew on that for a while.

Aztec Empire

The Aztecs were a brutal empire. They monstrously mistreated their own people. They believed one of their gods wanted freshly harvested human hearts for lunch. In 1489, the Aztecs recorded that they sacrificed eighty-four thousand people for their hearts in four days. The Spanish were also brutal in their treatment of the Aztecs. Between 1519 and 1521, the Spanish, under the leadership of Conquistador Hernán Cortés, conquered the Aztec Empire.

During the reign of King Montezuma II, the Aztecs had seen several bad omens. According to their religion, these omens mean that something bad was going to happen. Bad omens are everywhere today. As Americans, we need to act like civilized people and not amoral uncivilized savages.

Powerful people are always battling for control, nipping at the heels of freedom. There is nothing new under the sun. Thank God, I've not recently heard of anyone demanding fresh human hearts for lunch. Not yet!

China

After WWII, Mao Zedong's revolution created the People's Republic of China. He called the execution the Great Leap Forward, forcing peasant farmers to increase their output when the nation faced a famine. He beat, tortured, and starved them. In four short years, he killed forty-five million people, and their famine grew worse.

What a surprise! God did not overlook this evil, not for a second. This touches only one of China's many evil deeds. China has no respect today for human life. What would happen if we faced famine in our country? For certain, the laws of the ruling class will be in full force. Rest assured, the ruling class will not starve. Think about it.

China is up in our face now. The Biden presidency is up tight with this evil regime, working against America's benefit for sure. Actually, Biden will be gone soon, as he is only a puppet on the world stage, used by ruthless, power-hungry men. Apparently, he is either too greedy or stupid to see the handwriting on the wall (the Bible has a wonderful account of "the handwriting on the wall"). Kamala Harris, another far left puppet of the communist Bernie Sanders, who could be our president. What a frightful thought. She is a fool!

We are headed straight for a socialist country. When the one-world government enters the world stage, it rules three and a half years, then the Antichrist takes over the final three and half years of absolute horror until Jesus returns and rules on this earth a thousand years. Americans, hang on to your hats!

Napoleon

He was emperor of France from 1804 to 1814. Napoleon conquered much of Europe in the early nineteenth century. He brought about the death of millions of Europeans due to his barbaric conquest. He declared himself emperor and reinstated slavery only seven years after it was abolished. He ordered the mass execution of Haitians by gas. The Napoleon complex is a theorized inferiority complex. He was an evil little short man who basked in his fifteen minutes of glory.

Ancient History

There is nothing new under the sun. Think about ancient histories, conflicts, and peoples. You will find that our attitudes of covetousness and mistrust of neighbors differ little from ancient times. Tribes and clans comprised of likeminded people exemplify our natural bent toward the herd mentality. Today's political bent is first reeducation— alter our language, our societies, isolation, division, then hopefully total control. Anyone with half a brain would know that total unification is a fallacy. Even ancient history testifies to this, as we will see.

Those who spend their time watching the boob tube, soaking up massive liberal propaganda, and believing all the lies are surely lacking in maturity and judgment and possibility intelligence. Isn't it amazing how quickly a civilization can tumble backward? It takes a long time to build something worth having but just a moment in time to destroy. Rome's fall was followed by a thousand years of darkness. This is the most famous lesson to remember from ancient civilizations. Indoctrination is a means to an end. Man's constant pursuit of fame, fortune, and control is never the path to everlasting peace for any nation. Either we learn from government errors, personal mistakes, wrong thinking, and that of antiquity, or as fate decrees, we are destined to repeat the same old failures. Age and time is not a factor.

In an excerpt from a speech, Tacitus (AD 56–120), regarded as one of Rome's greatest statesmen, describes the torture of Christians:

Mockery of every sort added to their deaths. Covered with the skins of beast, they were torn by dogs and perished, or nailed to crosses, or doomed to the flames. Burnt, to serve as a nightly illumination when daylight had expired. Nero offered his garden for the spectacle, and was exhibiting a show in the circus, while he mingled with the people in the dress of a charioteer or stood aloft on a car. Hence, even for criminals who deserve extreme and exemplary punishment, there arose a feeling of compassion; for it was not, as it seemed, for the public good, but to glut one man's cruelty, that they were destroyed.

Romulus and Remus

Legend has it that Romulus and Remus, twin brothers who were also demigods, founded Rome on the River Tiber in 753 BC. They were born to a princess named Rhea Silvia, their father, the fierce Roman god of war, Mars. Can you imagine believing this absurdity? Over the next eight and a half centuries, it grew from a small town of pig farmers into a vast empire that stretched from England to Egypt and surrounded the Mediterranean Sea. Rome held on to these lands by letting them govern themselves.

Boudica

Boudica was the Celtic queen of the Iceni tribe of modern-day East Anglia. She led a revolt against Rome in 60-61 CE. The Iceni king Prasutagus, an independent ally of Rome, divided his estate between his daughters and the Roman emperor Nero Claudius Caesar (54–68 CE).

When Prasutagus died, however, Rome and the Iceni took his lands, lost their status as allies. When his wife, Boudica, objected to this action, she was flogged and her two daughters raped. She mounted a revolt against Rome, which left many ancient Romans dead.

Boudica was defeated at the Battle of Watling Street by the Roman governor Gaius Suetonius Paulinus (first century CE), chiefly by his judicious choice of the battlefield and allowing her army to cut off its own escape route by encircling their rear with wagons, animals, and families. Boudicca is said to have committed suicide by poisoning herself after her defeat. There are two versions of this story by Roman historians. Tacitus claims the revolt sprang from the ill treatment of the Iceni following Prasutagus's death, while Dio writes the cause of the uprising was a dispute over a loan.

Etruscans

The Romans were not the first people to live in ancient Italy. The Etruscans date back to the eighth century BC. The Greeks shared the peninsula in the south. Beyond that, scholars have debated for hundreds of years the origin of the Etruscans. Some believe they are of Turkish descent. The Etruscans gained a reputation in antiquity for being party-loving pushovers when it came to warfare. But who knows. Etruscans must be pieced together from what little remains of their culture.

The Etruscans grew into a complex, sophisticated society just north of Rome. The Etruscan government began as a monarchy then eventually into an oligarchy, ruled by members of society. Oligarchs rule many societies today. The Etruscans were a polytheistic society of all sorts of gods thought to govern everyday life. The Etruscans were famous for their omen-reading from birds and feather; in time, all became highly prized members of Roman households.

After 650 BC, the Etruscans dominated Italy in trade, including imported slaves. The people fought each other, competed over resources and trade routes. The Etruscans were most famous for their art, gold, tomb paintings, pottery, and bronze works—mostly dating to the early seventh century BC. Ancient Rome owes about everything creative to the Etruscans. The Roman Empire began absorbing the Etruscans in 396 BC.

The Etruscans, as a polytheistic society selecting their own gods, has proved to be nothing more than absurdity. To beat the system, simply find a god that agrees with you and cash in. If that didn't work, call in a few feathered friends. Once more, "there is nothing new under sun," including disgruntled societies and slave trading that has never ceased to exist. The Etruscans society consisted of slaves. Their art revealed social attitudes, depicting slaves in wall paintings as of smaller stature than citizens. The elite members of society easily identified from the mass of ordinary citizens by their clothes, hats, and various staffs of authority.

CHAPTER 19

Elites

Elites in our country own several mansions, private jets, and huge private yachts to cruise around the world in. Why should we look to these men as our leaders? Fortunes came from inherited money, self-made from honest dealings and from illicit enterprises. Money rules the world and always has. Those who have it could care less where it came from. One day soon, there will no longer be a middle class, only the very rich and the very poor. All you hell-raising Marxist and Democratic jerks, ask for it and you will eventually get it. I trust all the uninformed will enjoy writhing in gutter slime. This is where you may live if you live at all.

Washington DC

John Kerry's wife, Teresa, is well-educated and is fluent in seven languages. She is apparently very intelligent.

Teresa became an American citizen in 1971. CNN reported Teresa met her first husband, John Heinz, while a student in Geneva. The couple married in 1966 and had three sons. John Heinz was heir to a considerable fortune, the H. J. Heinz company. A Republican, Heinz was elected to congress in 1971 to 1977, then served as senator in 1977 until his death in a helicopter crash in 1991. Teresa inherited $700 million. Teresa Heinz chose to remain a Republican after marrying Kerry, a Democrat. She switched parties in 2002.

After Kerry graduated from Yale, he enlisted in the US Navy, serving in Vietnam. There is some controversy about Kerry's war service. Here it is! The Purple Heart. John Kerry had three Purple Hearts from shrapnel wounds. None of them took him off duty. The Purple Hearts were coming down in boxes. The Vietnam War did not consider a wound's severity and specified only that injuries had to suffered in action against an enemy. Two members on Kerry's Swift Boat claim that the wound was not from enemy fire but from shrapnel of a grenade he fired himself.

On the night in question, Kerry was not on a boat but on a fifteen-foot skimmer. Kerry opened fire on suspected guerrillas on the shore. During this encounter, Kerry suffered a shrapnel wound in the left arm above the elbow. Kerry has stated that he doesn't know where the shrapnel came from.

Admiral William Schachte, then a lieutenant, stated that he regularly led training missions for recently arrived officers such as Kerry. At the time, he described Kerry as a rookie. One tactic described by Schachte was for a Swift

Boat to tow the skimmer to the target area and wait nearby. The skimmer, manned by three people, "would go in, draw fire and get out immediately." The waiting Swift boat or air support would attack the enemies thus detected. Schachte stated that he was on the skimmer with one other enlistee the night Kerry was injured. Schachte popped a flare after detecting movement and opened fire. He stated that there was no return fire and that Kerry was *nicked* by a fragment from a grenade he launched and fired himself. There are those who dispute the incident.

John Kerry's mother was Rosemary Isabel Forbes, born in Paris, France, of the wealthy Boston Forbes and descendent of John Winthrop, first governor of Massachusetts. The Forbes family's fortune originates from trading opium and tea between North America and China in the nineteenth century, plus other investments in the same period. Well, do tell! John Kerry's (Mr. Ketchup) family were drug dealers. Apparently, money makes you look respectable no matter how you acquired it. The point in bringing this story to light is to say that money marries money. Who knows, I may have fallen into that trap if given the opportunity, and I was.

Washington is no longer about lawmaking. It's about moneymaking. Washington is broken because outside special interest groups bribe politicians. The reverse is true; politicians have developed a new set of brass-knuckle legislative tactics designed to extort wealthy industries and donors into forking over big donations of cash that lawmakers often funnel into the pockets of their friends and family.

Schweizer explains how a new corruption has taken hold, involving larger sums of money than ever before. Stuffing tens of thousands of dollars into a freezer has morphed into multibillion-dollar equity deals done in the dark corners of the world.

President Donald Trump's children have made front pages across the world for their dicey transactions. However, the media has barely looked into questionable deals made by those close to Barack Obama, Joe Biden, John Kerry, Mitch McConnel, and lesser-known politicians who have been in the game.

This is a relatively new phenomenon in the United States. But for relatives of some prominent political families, we may already be talking about hundreds of millions of dollars. *Secret Empires* by Peter Schweizer was deeply researched and packed with shocking revelations, identifying public servants who cannot be trusted. He provides a path toward a more accountable government.

Schweizer has written other books that will enlighten the reader on Washington, DC, corruption.

The Democratic party continues their desperate pursuit to discredit President Trump at the cost to taxpayers of multimillions of dollars. Donald Trump is not a politician; he is a self-made businessman. He drew no salary, making him a true American looking out for our country, our Constitution, and our way of life to no avail. The Democratic pack of hungry wolves have wasted years and millions of dollars attempting to expose Trump's finances and discredit him in a thousand ways. His finances are none of our business.

Millions of wasted dollars would feed a multitude of hungry people. No one complained about that ugly government waste. Trump did. He did something about it and stepped on lots of toes in the process. The knee-jerking public fanatically chose sides, swearing by its candidate while alienating friends. Some people didn't vote for Trump because they could not stand the man. Is this considered logic? If they had given the matter even a little thought, they would have cheered his policies, never mind the man. It is a sad state of affairs when the president of the United States cannot deliver a speech without a script and still mess up. Every word President Biden says is scripted. Any excuse is a lame excuse for putting a mentally impaired socialist in office. A closed-minded public absent of sound reason is dangerous.

The Biden crime family was in no way wealthy before entering Washington politics. Unlike Trump, Biden has been at the political trough his entire adult life. He never fails to mention his working-class family. So politics generated the Biden millions, or was it the tooth fairy? The Bidens are now in bed with the communist Chinese and the Russians and immediately vetoed all the good things Trump did for America. President Trump stopped lining the pockets of foreign entities who hate America. What a novel idea! The Biden family hasn't lost a single minute lining their pockets. If anyone disbelieves this account of the Bidens, the facts are there for those who want the truth brought to light. Our debt doubled or tripled during the Obama administration, and it just keeps growing. It would not surprise me if Obama still held the reins of the Democratic party. Joe Biden doesn't lead anything.

Biden is president in name only—a dreadful thought! There is no conceivable way our country can ever get out of debt, and it keeps on growing. The feds are printing money like crazy. When Biden gets through, America will sink at warp speed further and further into debt, inflation, and darkness; remember Germany.

Seven years of biblical tribulation is primed and ready, waiting in the wings. Then evil will cover the globe faster and thicker than fleas on a dog's back. Cannot say exactly when this will happen, just that the signs are there for all who care to see. You only know what you know.

CHAPTER 20

Empires

Throughout history, empire builders have come into being, then cease to exist. The road to empire building has never changed, only the names and faces differ. Empires grow by acquiring or conquering neighboring territories; stabilizing the region; establishing politics, speech, religion or lack of; then hopefully, peace and prosperity will occur. Societies have short memories. When the economy is flourishing and all things are rosy, humanity never considers their inception may have derive through evil intent. Who cares!

Unfortunately, like all human institutions, they will become corrupt over time, and as we have seen, history proves this point. All powers desperately cling to control and suppress any dissidence within to maintain the stability. The climb up a ladder is long, but the fall down takes mere seconds.

Wake up, America! This is happening to us this very moment. The Constitution of the United States of America guarantees us freedom of speech. The buffoons out to destroy our country stomp on the word *freedom*. When our speech is deemed inadmissible to the corrupt degenerates policing our thoughts and words, we simply have the power to proclaim the truth. Americans, let us dispose of this evil. Now! I don't recall attack dogs mentioned in the first amendment! Today, we have listeners who delete anything deemed politically incorrect or in disagreement with the present agenda of changing our country. Privacy no longer exists. A few billionaire oligarchs are a fact to be reckoned with. They plan to rule. What goes around, comes around. Heard a woman say on TV that anyone who voted for Trump needs to be interned and reprogrammed. I think her name was Joy. This kind of ignorant speech would be laughable if it weren't so sinister. There is nothing new under the sun. We did intern the Japanese during WWII for their criminal, inhuman treatment of prisoners for very different reasons.

During the Communist era in East Germany, the ruling elite adopted a song with the uncompromising line, "The Party, the Party, which is always right." Today's Chinese Communist Party is not quite so blunt. A resolution on China's history issued by the CCP strikes a more nuanced note: "The Party is great not because it never makes mistakes, but because it always owns up to its errors, actively engages in criticism and self-criticism, and has the courage to confront problems and reform itself." What a crock! From inception, Chinese Communists were liars, and nothing has changed. To this day, China has absolutely no respect for human rights. Once the world's evil-begotten wealth begins to dissipate, the chickens will have no place to roost.

By 1985, one-third of the world's population lived under a Marxist-Leninist system of government in one form or another. All you lazy bums who mostly avoid work can now cash in. The government will confiscate the peoples' property and give a little piece of it to other bums in the name of equality. This is beyond stupid.

Tiananmen Square

Who can forget the Tiananmen Square Massacre? In May 1989, nearly a million Chinese, mostly young students, crowded into Central Beijing to protest for greater democracy and called for the resignation of Chinese Communist Party leaders deemed to be repressive. For three weeks, the protesters never let up. On June 4, 1989, Chinese troops stormed Tiananmen Square, firing indiscriminately into the crowds. The people fought back to no avail. An estimated three hundred, and perhaps thousands, had been killed, and as many as ten thousand were arrested. This was 1989 and not ancient history; yes, there is nothing new under the sun. Pray that our nation's issues will never escalate into a Tiananmen Square Massacre. It's possible! Think about it!

Sometime after the massacre, my granddaughter Kristen joined a group headed for Beijing to pray for the people and the city. Describing themselves as tourists, they walked around the city, praying in silence. We were so proud of her but so happy when she came home in one piece. God called them to Beijing; He brought them home.

CHAPTER 21

Ancient Empires

Compare a few ancient societies that echo our own United States in modern history. I think you will be amazed; the playbooks are the same. The only thing ancient civilizations lacked was our modern technology with the means to reach anywhere in the world in seconds.

Rome

Rome was founded in 753 BC. Rome's era as a monarchy ended in 509 BC, overthrown by the seventh king, Lucius Tarquinius Superbus. He was a cruel and tyrannical king compared to his benevolent predecessors. A popular uprising was said to have arisen over the rape of a virtuous nobility by the king's son. A political revolution overthrew the Roman monarchy around 509 BC. Then 122 years later, unrest is once more on the way!

The Gauls (Gallic) destroyed much of Rome's historical records when they sacked the city after the Battle of the Allia in 387 BC. Anything left was eventually lost to time or theft. With no contemporary records of the kingdom existing, all accounts of the king were carefully questioned. Some historians believed that Rome was under the influence of the Etruscans for about a century. The Etruscans were great engineers and the second greatest impact on Roman development, only surpassed by the Greeks. Expanding further south, the Etruscans came into direct contact with the Greeks and initially had success in conflict with the Greeks, after which, Etruria went into a decline. Taking advantage of this, Rome rebelled and gained independence from the Etruscans around 599 BC.

Rome also abandoned the monarchy in favor of a republic system based on a senate with popular assemblies, which ensured political participation for most of the freemen and elected magistrates annually. The Etruscans left a lasting influence on Rome.

Rome first became a republic in 509 BCE. The Roman Republic lasted for several centuries before tensions within the government began to tear it apart. Does this not sound painfully familiar? Civil wars, different loyalties, eventually turned the republic into an Empire. A consul held the highest elected political office of the republic. Each year the citizens elected two consuls—rulers—to serve jointly for a one-year term. During times of war, the primary qualification of consul was military skill and reputation.

Many aspects of Roman law and the Roman constitution are still used today in America's laws. These include concepts like checks and balances, vetoes, separation of powers, term limits, and regular elections. Many of these concepts serve as the foundation of today's modern democratic government. What happened to checks and balances and term limits?

Roman law is also responsible for creating a legal code written down, which protected the rights of all citizens. What happened to our rights? What happened to innocent until proven guilty? Volumes could be written on the failures of our government. These laws are just and righteous. It's the bums in Washington who need to be replaced, not our laws. Beware of who or what you license power to over our nation and its people. Our freedoms hang in the balance this very moment.

Hannibal

Hannibal Barca, 183–47 BC, was a Carthaginian general and political leader who commanded Carthage's main forces against the Roman Republic during the Second Punic War. Hannibal is widely considered one of the greatest military commanders in human history. In 218 BC, Hannibal marched through the Pyrenees mountains toward Gaul (Southern France) with more than one hundred thousand troops and forty war elephants.

The Roman general Publius Cornelius attempted to confront Hannibal at the Rhône River, but Hannibal had already crossed it and was on his way to the Alps. He faced numerous guerrilla attacks before finally exiting the Alps with just twenty thousand infantry, six thousand cavalry, and all forty elephants. He was able to inflict heavy casualties. He got within three miles of the capital before a stalemate ensued.

Hannibal spent the next several years in politics. Then the Romans became concerned about Hannibal's growing power and in 195 BC demanded he retire. Hannibal moved to Ephesus and became a military adviser. Around 183 BC, Hannibal took his own life by ingesting a vial of poison.

Julius Caesar

Julius Caesar first became dictator in 49 BC but resigned within eleven days. In 48 BC, he was reappointed dictator for an indefinite period, then in 46 BC, appointed for ten years. It is safe to say that slavery was accepted throughout all Roman societies. People, like sheep, are going to live and do whatever they do. Hopefully, all societies will eventually reject tyrannical rule. Then what? Who is to blame? The populists will always look elsewhere to place blame, never once considering the role they played in the destruction of a nation. Yesterday is history; slavery is not. Like slavery, dipping snuff was a socially accepted habit in my grandmothers' generation, but don't blame me if snuff turned out to be lethal and they all died from dipping. People make choices.

Julius Caesar invaded Britain in 56 BC because he wanted to gain the glory of a victory beyond the great ocean, and he believed that Britain was full of silver and booty to be plundered. This greedy attempt failed. He did no more than force his way onto shore. He returned empty-handed. Then in 54 BC, he tried again, this time with five legions, and succeeded. There was no silver or booty found in Britain, only Caesar's greed left behind.

Claudius

Claudius was born August 1, 10 BC in Laudanum (modern-day Lyon), France. Claudius seized his chance in AD 43. He sent four legions across the sea to invade Britain. This time, success. Vespasian stormed Maiden Castle, Hod Hill, with such ruthless efficiency that the catapult bolts used to subdue them are still dug out of the ground today. Claudius entered Colchester in triumph, where he founded a temple there, containing a fine bronze statue of himself, and established a legionary fortress there. Pride is infectious. He remained in Britain for only sixteen days. It took another thirty years to conquer the rest of the island.

It has been said that Rome conquered an empire in a fit of absentmindedness. The invasion of Britain was to further a political career. Political self-centered men, seeking glory at the expense of others, have not changed since the beginning of time. Political masterminds of today have their greedy sights on America. Wake up, people! Americans must rise up against any form of one-world government, total central control.

The Roman state grew in both size and power. Though the Gaul's sacked and burned Rome in 390 BC, the Romans rebounded, eventually gaining control of the entire Italian peninsula by 264 BC. Then Rome fought a series of wars, eventually gaining control of Sicily, the Mediterranean islands, and modern-day Spain. Then when Julius Caesar came along, he led Roman soldiers into Northwest Europe. In addition to pushing Rome's reach across Europe, Caesar also heralded the end of the *republic* and the beginning of the empire and to the republic of which it stands. Republic is a familiar word in our American Constitution. Think about the end results threatening our republic today.

After Caesar declared himself dictator for life in 44 BC, he didn't last long. Senators murdered him in 44 BC. The republic fell for good when his great-nephew Augustus Caesar declared himself emperor in 27 BC. Now the state of Rome was officially the Roman Empire. In 212, the Roman Empire extended citizenship to all free people. Free women had fewer rights than males.

Roman men were free to enjoy sex with other males without a perceived loss of masculinity or social status as long as they took the dominant role. Isn't this absurd? What about the catamites, pubescent boys, nude, with legs and arms strapped, swinging in booths at the Colosseum. Pay for sex. Apparently, a profitable business. These children were both black and white and owned by their promoters. This is unconscionable! If a man liked anal or oral sex, then he could have that form of sex with his slave. We are rapidly following in the footsteps of Rome. It only takes a moment in time for a heart to become corrupt.

Nero

Nero was a real charmer. After kicking his pregnant wife to death, Nero castrated a boy (Sporous) who resembled her and took him as his wife. "After Nero's suicide, Sporous was taken to the care of the Praetorian prefect Nymphidius Sabinus. Nymphidius treated Sporous as a wife and called him Poppaea. Nymphidius tried to make himself emperor but was killed by his own guardsmen. Then Sporous became involved with Otho, the second of a rapid, violent succession of four emperors who vied for power during the chaos that followed Nero's death" (Wikipedia). No doubt, Rome was steeped in every form of sin. One must assume this detestable behavior was acceptable in Roman society. We are not yet a pagan society. What assures us the same proclivity in our country will not eventually reach this same depth of depravity?

Rome was a pagan society, worshiping a pantheon of Roman and Greek deities. Romans consulted the deities about everything. Some Roman emperors claimed descent from demigods such as Hercules. The subjects were encouraged to think of their rulers as semidivine figures, as is the case from antiquity and something our present-day senseless idiots may hope to achieve.

Slavery was deeply woven into the fabric of Roman society. As the Roman Empire expanded, they often captured slaves from new lands they conquered. Other slaves were bought from slave traders and pirates who captured people from foreign lands and brought them to Rome. Children of slaves also became slaves. During the early days, as many as one third of the people in Rome were enslaved. Romans had the right to beat their slaves. Runaways were severely punished or killed. Emperor Romulus Augustulus, 475–476, gave Roman fathers the right to sell their children into slavery. Beastly people!

Spartacus

The slaves banded together and rebelled several times during the history of Rome, led by the gladiator Spartacus (73–71 BCE). The Third Servile War was the largest slave revolt against Rome. Gladiators were drawn from various sources but chiefly slaves and criminals. With an army in the tens of thousands marching up and down the peninsula, Spartacus defeated Roman forces over half a dozen times. He was finally killed in battle in 71 BC. The history of Spartacus is interesting and worth studying.

Why does Roman slavery not enrage the Black Lives Matter gang? Why are they not over there tearing up Italy? Why? Because they have no idea about true black history from antiquity forward. They are steeped in Marxist doctrine. Actually, reparation is not a cure for anything coming down today or yesterday. In fact, it's a lie. Reparation is like throwing money down the Black Hole of Calcutta, a wretched prison cell. Throwing money at a society never solved its ills. Will money bring a person to forgiveness of past and future injustices? I don't think so. When our needs are met today, there is still tomorrow. True forgiveness feeds the soul and heals wounds.

Constantine

Emperor Constantine (AD 306–337) and his mother, Helena Augusta, converted to Christianity. Then all of Rome followed suit. It was the popular thing to do at the time. Usually, when a king or emperor said squat, everybody squats. After issuing the Edict of Milan in 313, this proclamation legalized Christianity and allowed for freedom of worship throughout the empire. He abolished the death penalty of crucifixion. He abolished gladiatorial games in 325 AD but without much effect since they were again abolished by the emperor Honorius (393–423) and may have continued for a century after that. Old habits are hard to break.

Constantine's father, Constantius Chlorus, was an officer in the Roman Army. Constantine's mother was from humble beginnings; it is unknown whether she was the wife or concubine. In 289, Constantine's father left Helena to marry the stepdaughter of Maximian the Western Roman emperor. He was elevated to deputy emperor under Maximian in 293. Now this self-centered human being became emperor in 305. This was his goal from the beginning. Constantine's father died in battle, and his son was declared emperor by his troops. During a period of civil war, Constantine defended his position. Accounts of his life state that following a vision, he had ordered a Christian symbol painted on his soldiers' shields. Under this emblem, he was successful in battle and entered Rome.

As the Western Roman emperor, Constantine soon used his power to address the status of Christianity. He established religious tolerance, allowing for freedom of worship throughout the empire. He passed a law ordering the observance of Sunday as a holy day. Sunday was another workday in the Roman Empire until Constantine issued a civil decree making Sunday a day of rest, upon the venerable day of the pagan sun god Ra, not built upon Jesus's resurrection.

Christianity became the official religion of Rome and its provinces, including Egypt. He erected great basilicas for Christianity. Along with his mother, Helena, they declared many places as Christian holy sites. The bones of the apostle Peter supposedly rest on Vatican Hill. The Jesus tomb in Jerusalem and the place of Jesus's birth are all holy sites. The authenticity of these sites is questionable. I've been inside the very small tomb-like garden—not authentic—yet I had a genuine sense of reverence once inside the tomb. We visited a type of manger in Bethlehem and the approximate area of Jesus's birth. These two sites were highlights of our visit. The authenticity of some sites is questionable, but that doesn't really matter. I am blessed to have been to Jerusalem, Bethlehem, Masada, the Dead Sea, and throughout the Holy Land's authentic sites. Just walking in the footsteps of Jesus made His life more alive than ever before. While on the Mount of Olives, the *ham* in me perked up. I had my picture taken perched upon a camel's back. Quite a thrill.

To the southeast is the city's earliest known water source, Gihon Spring. The spring brought water uphill (under natural pressure) into the fortified walls of the lower city, then later into the Old City via a well-hidden and formerly guarded tunnel. We visited this ancient authentic well below the city of Jerusalem. The well still supplies the city's water. The air was very cold down there, as was the water.

The most disturbing site we visited was underneath the City of Jerusalem, where Roman soldiers took turns torturing Jesus. They played "The Game of Kings," which was so brutal they were only allowed to play it once a year. Soldiers could choose the victim. Mel Gibson's *Passion of the Christ* depicted this scene. A soldier was seated at a table with an assortment of instruments of torture. I believe Satan was running around behind the crowd, taking it all in. Standing on ground where this may have happened brought tears to my eyes. Man's inhumanity to man is beyond rampant in our world today. You only know what you know.

Standing there in the midst of evil brought a flood of tears to my eyes. Man's inhumanity to man has never ceased to exist and should never be ignored by decent people. There is no way I have seen it all but I'm most grateful for what I am blessed to have experienced. Hopefully, I will return one day. Wouldn't trade my Jerusalem experience for anything. Amen!

Alexandre the Great took control of Jerusalem in 332 BC. Over the next several hundred years, the city was conquered and ruled by different groups, including the Romans, Persians, Arabs, Fatimids, Seljuk Turks, Crusaders, Egyptians, Mamluks, and Islamists. Jerusalem is considered the navel of the world, a place where untold numbers of Jews, Muslims, and Christians come looking for God. Billions more would come from afar. Over one hundred battles would be fought in the city's name. History of the city from such towering figures as Abraham, King David, Jesus, Muhammad, and others can still be told from stones of archaeology and oral traditions passed down for millennia and from the text of three great religions.

Masada

Another unforgettable excursion was the Dead Sea and taking a lift up to Masada. Masada was an ancient stone fortress in Israel, located high above the Dead Sea on a tall rocky mesa. Masada is located on the edge of the Judean desert, on cliffs made of chalk, dolomite, and marl strata about 1,300 feet above the Dead Sea. Because of the desert climate, the surrounding area is virtually uninhabited and underdeveloped. Because of the lake's extreme salinity, the only thing that lives in the sea is bacteria.

I will never forget the awesome views of a sea surrounded by barren lands as seen from atop Masada. No green, only soft pastels as far as the eye could see. A warm, dry breeze gently gliding across the mesa sealed the whole enchanting scene firmly in my mind's eye. God willing, I hope to someday capture the moment on canvas.

There was no water in the desert. Once a year, there were flash floods in the desert. The people dammed up an area to catch water enough for survival. They carried water in earthen jars up the steep passageways to the top. The arid air preserved fruit and nuts for a thousand years. Brave people will take giant steps to survive.

The Great Revolt of the Jews against the Romans broke out in AD 60. A group of Jewish people known as the Sicarii took over the Masada complex. In AD 70, with Jerusalem in ruins, the Romans turned their attention to taking down Masada, the last community in Judea. After many failed attempts, the Romans built a ramp on the side of the mountain made of earth and wood then catapulted the walls. Before the Romans reached the top, all the people had committed suicide, except for one woman left to tell the story. These Jewish people were intelligent, strong, and brave. Another picture of eliminating people who challenge the authorities. The Romans must have been disappointed when met with nothing but dead bodies. The Sicarii decided that death by their own hand was better than anything the Romans planned. Hollywood made a wonderful movie worth seeing, *Masada*. I own this movie. "You only know what you know."

Persia

Native Egyptian rule lasted until the conquest by the Achaemenid Empire in the sixth century BC. The Achaemenid Empire (modern-day Iraq) was the first Persian empire and one of the largest empires ever in history. Founded by Cyrus the Great, the empire is notable for a centralized bureaucracy, building roads, a postal system, use of an official language, and developed civil service.

On the whole, slavery in the Achaemenid empire was only small numbers in relation to the number of free persons. Usually, captives were prisoners of war recruited from those who rebelled against Achaemenid rule. Slavery was a common institution in Safavid Iran (ancient Persia). Slaves were employed on many levels of society throughout the Persian Empire (600 BC–20th Century AD). African slaves were imported by the East African slave trade across the Indian Ocean. White slaves were provided through warfare, slave raids, and punitive expeditions in Caucasus and Northern Iran. This provided for Christian Armenian, Georgian, Circassians, and for Muslim Iranians captured in slave raids by the Turkmens. Actually, all Persian people were slaves to the king.

Persian decline is attributed to heavy tax burdens and the failure to establish a national identity among its subjects from different nations. Once again, painfully familiar. Together, American citizens have established a national identity for all legal citizens. Those who enter legally are welcome. However, our open southern border inundated with illegals from across the globe are not welcome. Many have no respect for the law or for our law-abiding citizens.

Eventually, America may not have a national identity if left up to the Biden administration and his goons controlling Washington. Why is this not obvious to all the lamebrains who voted for Biden? Biden's henchmen brazenly get on TV, announcing the borders are closed and with a straight face! I live in Texas. I have eyes. I see the tidal wave of undocumented people roaring across our borders like a deadly tsunami. The government drops busloads and planeloads of them off in cities and towns throughout America. Dallas has more than its share stuffed in the

Kay Bailey Hutchison Convention Center. Go peddle your
lies elsewhere. Many are hardened criminals, drug dealers
expelled by their own government. Let America deal with
them! I believe we will live to regret this stupid move.

Carthaginian Empire

The Carthaginian Empire, 650–146 BCE. Carthage
was an ancient Phoenician city-state and civilization
located in present day Tunisia on the north coast of Africa.
Founded around 814 BC as a colony of Tyre, within centuries it became the center of the Carthaginian Empire, a
major commercial and maritime power that dominated the
Western Mediterranean until the mid-third century BC.

The aristocracy of Carthage was not, as in many
ancient societies, based on land ownership but wealth,
pure and simple. This meant that enterprising individuals
were able to exploit the market conditions of the city where
goods were exported, imported, and manufactured. These
were the aristocrats who dominated all of the important
political and religious positions. Check this out—Aristotle
commenting on Carthage: "a preoccupation with wealth
would lead inevitably to a self-centered oligarchy dominat-
ing society." Bravo, Aristotle, you finally ring my bell.

Below this stratum was a cosmopolitan mix of artisans,
laborers, mercenaries, slaves, and foreigners from across the
Mediterranean. It's doubtful today that a few millions will
be enough money to keep you out of the lower strata. It
will take trillions.

Carthaginian slaves were either conquered peoples or bought from slave markets and used for all manner of tasks, professional or menial, in the city and in the countryside, as well as in the navy during the Punic Wars.

Despite the importance of such goddesses as Tanit Astarte in the Carthaginian religion and the myth of the city's founding by Queen Dido, women were not granted citizenship and could not participate in the political life of the city; they remained silent. Who knows, the power-hungry idiots hoping to rule the world may try that little trick on us. Well, good luck.

Hannibal Barca, one of the greatest minds in the ancient world, was a Carthaginian general who was considered to be one of the great military leaders in history. He held a lifelong grudge against Rome. In 218 BC, Hannibal marched his troops, including cavalry and African war elephants, across a high pass in the Alps to strike at Rome from the north of the Italian peninsula. One of the greatest military feats in history. So ended the second Punic war, with Rome the victor.

Hannibal believed Italians were suffering under the Roman yoke. And so they were! He enjoyed an unbroken string of victories on the battlefield, including the total destruction of a Roman army at Cannae in 216. Hannibal did not attract enough allies to bring bout Rome's defeat. Skirmishing continued for fifteen years. Then the paranoid Romans provoked a third Punic war against the helpless Carthaginians that led to the total destruction of their civilization. America is not helpless. We must stay aware of our enemies within who plot to destroy our country. It's all about empowering the few. Nothing new under the sun.

Kushite Empire

The Kushite Empire (Nubian Dynasty), established and ended: 760–656 BC. The founding country was ancient Egypt, ruled by the Nubians from the kingdom of Kush (Northern Sudan and Southern Egypt). The war brought together Upper and Lower Egypt and Kush, forming the largest Egyptian empire since the New Kingdom (circa 1550–1077 BC). Under Piaye, the construction of pyramids revived, and he built the oldest pyramid at the royal burial site of EL-Kurru and expanded the temple of Amun at Jebel Barkal. They were also attempting to regain parts of Egypt from the Assyrians but were unsuccessful. And the plot continues. Slaves were the builders.

Think about this. Kush is a Hebrew name. According to biblical history, Kush was the eldest son of Ham, who was the eldest son of Noah. Kush was the brother of Canaan (land of Canaan), Mizraim (Egypt), and Put (Ethiopia). Kush was the father of the biblical Nimrod; Noah was his grandfather (Genesis 10:6 and 1 Chronicles 1:8). The story of Nimrod is most interesting and well worth reading. He was the founder and king of Babylon. Nimrod built the Tower of Babel, the center of a city they thought would reach to the heavens. At that time all people spoke the same language (Genesis 11:1–9); explains why the world's people now speak different languages. God had a purpose. The world would have you believe this is a myth. Just like all the other power-hungry men since, Nimrod wanted control, so God put a stop to it.

Egypt

There were three ancient empires before the Egyptian Empire came into power. As these ancient civilizations grew, so did their sphere of power and their desire to conquer near and distance lands. These first empires ruled over the same land, eventually replacing one another as they fell. What a circus that must have been. "Who's on first?" (the Three Stooges).

To keep the bloodline pure, Pharaohs married their sisters or half-sisters, and Pharaoh Akhenaten married his own daughters. Early on, the rulers married in an effort to establish the legitimacy of their dynasty by linking it to the upper classes of Memphis, which was then Egypt's capital.

Interesting to note that Egyptians believed an individual life mattered enough to be remembered. Reminds me of our Hutchison clan. Also interesting to note that Egyptians believe that one's life was an eternal journey; therefore, death was only a transition inspiring the people to try and make their lives worth living. These worthy thoughts create worthy ambitions.

As Christians, we believe in life after death, and in that light, life is an eternal journey. Christians endeavor to live a grateful life on earth as good witness for Christ's finished work on the cross. Our journey is guided by the

Holy Spirit (the Lord's Spirit), who directs our steps. We are assured of eternal life through Jesus Christ and not contingent upon anything we do. Don't turn your nose up to this vital truth as entry to eternal life. Intelligent people seek. "Seek and you shall find, knock and it will be opened unto you" (Matthew 7:7–8, Luke 11:9–10).

The ancient Egyptians first established their kingdom around 3100 BC. Until its conquest by Alexander the Great in 332 BC, ancient Egypt was the preeminent civilization in the Mediterranean world. King Menes founded the capital of ancient Egypt at "white walls" (later known as Memphis). The capital would grow into a great metropolis that dominated Egyptian society. To the ancient Egyptians, the king was a godlike being, closely identified with the all-powerful god Horus.

Around 2630 BC, the third dynasty's King Djoser (zoser) asked Imhotep—an architect, priest, and healer—to design a funerary monument for him; the result was the world's first major stone building, the step pyramid near Memphis, later the Great Pyramid, named by classical historians as one of the Seven Wonders of the World. It took one hundred thousand slaves twenty years to build it. Now, how does the BLM crowd feel about that? Was this a great injustice? Why not go tear up Egypt? BLM refuses to acknowledge or more likely is unaware that one hundred thousand men were responsible for creating one of the Seven Wonders of the World. They were not running around destroying property, killing people, and screaming injustice and reparations. Their contributions to the world are to this day praised and appreciated. All you BLM idiots and supporters are so terribly misinformed; you are drowning in your own ignorance.

During the third and fourth dynasties, Egypt enjoyed a golden age of peace and prosperity. The pharaohs held absolute power and provided a stable central government. Eventually, the king's wealth steadily depleted, and his absolute power faltered (money rules) in the face of the growing influence of the nobility and the priesthood that grew around the sun god Ra. After the death of the sixth dynasty's King Pepi II that ruled for ninety-four years, the old kingdom period ended in chaos. The pyramids remain.

The nineteenth and twentieth dynasties, known as the Ramesside period, saw the restoration of the weakened Egyptian empire. The exodus of Moses and the Israelites occurred around 1440 BCE. In 525 BC, the Persian empire ruled the country under the same terms as Egyptian kings.

The Israelites were slaves in Egypt for four hundred years. The Jews had been in Egypt for generations. The Israelites had become so numerous that Pharaoh feared they would one day turn against the Egyptians. Gradually, he forced them to become slaves. But still fearful of an uprising, he ordered all infant males killed—terrible punishment. Pharaoh gave orders to the midwives that every son born, you shall cast into the river. Moses's mother put her baby boy in a reed basket then put the basket afloat among the reeds. The princess saw him, rescued baby Moses, and raised him as her son. He lived a privileged, educated life.

It is Moses who led the slaves in revolt and led them through the Red Sea, where God parted the waters. Once the Israelites safely reached the other side, the water began to close, drowning all the pursuing Egyptians. These are recorded historical facts, not fairy tales. *Exodus* is a biblical epic film about Moses and the Israelites leaving Egypt. Great movie!

After several more defeated empires a decade later, in 332 BC, Alexander the Great defeated the armies of the Persian Empire and conquered Egypt. The last ruler of Ptolemaic Egypt was the legendary Cleopatra until her death in 30 BC. Egypt then surrendered to the armies of Octavian. The conquest of Egypt by the Arabs in the seventh century AD, and the introduction of Islam would do away with the last outward aspects of ancient Egyptian culture. This brief synopsis doesn't do justice to the volumes written on the subject.

Christianity became the official religion of Rome and its provinces (including Egypt). In 380 CE, the emperor Theodosius issued the Edict of Thessalonica, which made Christianity, specifically Nicene Christianity, the official religion of the Roman Empire. Most other sects, deemed heretical, lost their legal status and had their property confiscated by the Roman state. This was the Roman Catholic Church.

For at least forty years, I dreamed of traveling through Egypt and made several attempts to join a group. Just could never gather up enough money at the time. I'm blessed to live in my imagination, so Egypt comes to me when I call. Praise God, I have gratefully managed to see more of the world than I ever dreamed possible.

Greece

Ancient Greek history lasted from the Dark Ages to the end of antiquity 12 BC–AD 600. The conquests of Alexander the Great of Macedonia spread Hellenistic civilization from the Western Mediterranean to Central Asia. The Hellenistic period ended with the Eastern Mediterranean world by the Roman Republic and the annexation of the Roman province of Macedonia in Roman Greece. Just more conquer and defeat.

The number of slaves in ancient Greece is estimated to have been eighty thousand to one hundred thousand. One fourth of the Athenians were slaves. It is estimated that the majority of Athenian citizens owned at least one slave. There were two groups of slaves. The first being born into captivity, while the second was captured or acquired as a result of war or piracy. They were otherwise free human beings enslaved as a result of coincidence. Having slaves was a universally accepted phenomenon for Greeks, and they grew up with their slaves forming a kind of friendship with them. Even the greatest thinkers could not imagine a world free of slavery interwoven into Greek culture.

Besides the sin of slavery in ancient Greece, pederasty was a socially acknowledged romantic relationship between an adult male and an adolescent youth. *Pederasty*, meaning "boy love." The roots of Greek pederasty lie in the tribal past of Greece. When it came time for a young boy to embrace the age group of the adult and to "become a man," he would leave the tribe in the company of an older man for a period of time that constitute a rite of passage. The boy was educated in the ways of Greek life and the responsibilities of adulthood. This practice evolved into the commonly known form of Greek pederasty. It is my opinion the adult male teacher found a way to earn money and at the same time legally satisfy his own illicit sexual desires at the expense of young men.

Societies have continued to sink lower and lower into the depths of this sin. Now, sex trafficking children is acceptable in many countries. America tops the list for pornography production and sales. Sexual perversion is rampant in the Roman Catholic priesthood and systematically covered up by the Vatican.

The Sacred Band of Thebes, a separate military unit made up of pairs of male lovers, is usually considered the prime example of how the ancient Greeks used love between soldiers in a troop to boost their fighting spirit. This all stems from ancient Greek mythology. It is nothing more than appealing to the flesh, which stems from the deceiver, Satan. Satan is not a myth.

Two-inch statues of ugly little men with giant penises larger than the body sold everywhere in the Plaka. A big seller. I fail to see the humor. Greek men are known to be bisexual and pedophiles. By now, they must claim it's in their DNA. I was alone in the Plaka beneath the city of Athens, killing time between my flight to Germany. Coming from Israel, Athens was an overnight stay between flights. Couldn't wait to get out of that place for fear of what else I might encounter. Got ripped off by a cab driver from the airport to the hotel.

On an earlier Holy Land tour with my sister, we toured Athens, explored the Parthenon ruins and Greek Isles by ship on the beautiful Aegean Sea. Maybe the most beautiful water of all the seas. A favorite was the ruins of the ancient port city of Ephesus. We docked at Kuşadasi, Turkey, then a short bus ride to Ephesus. Ephesus in its prime was a beautiful port city with white marble streets, walkways, and walls culminating along the clear azure-blue sea, where ships lined the harbor. What a picture! By now the sea was not visible from land. We walked through the ruins of marble streets and sidewalks lined with marble walls. The ruins of a huge two-story structure was the white marble library. The grand theater of Ephesus encircled a stage, mostly in ruins. This was the largest theater in Asia Minor with accommodations for twenty-five thousand people and one thousand standing places, two-story at one time. The theater served for dramatic performances, social, political, economic, religious nature, and gladiator games. The ancient city of Ephesus must have been a beautiful, remarkable sight.

This theater is mentioned in Acts 19. A riot was started against the apostle Paul in AD 56 by Demetrius the silversmith. He provoked his fellow craftsmen to a public outcry against Paul. Demetrius made silver statues of Artemis and feared Paul's teaching would destroy his business. He went around yelling, "Great is Artemis!" Artemis was said to have fallen from the sky. The Ephesians and people throughout the known world worshipped the goddess Artemis. Business was good. Copies of the Artemis cult statues have been excavated in many part of the Roman Empire. The Ephesians worshipped Artemis for fertility. Depictions mirror this, with the deity wearing a string of eggs as breasts around her shoulders and chest. She was the most worshiped deity in Asia. Hundreds of eunuch priest, virgin priestesses, and religious prostitutes served her. Worship rituals were quite erotic—the promise of fertility, long life, sexual fulfilment, protection during childbearing. Devotees came from all over the world to worship and celebrate her festivals. Huge processions honored her statues. The temple was one of the Seven Wonders of the Ancient World.

In the modern era, concerts take place in the Ephesus theater. Elton John, Mikis Theodorakis, Ray Charles, Sting, Diana Ross, and others performed on this ancient stage.

Back aboard the ship, we twisted and turned through a labyrinth of tiny isles and inlets to the island of Patmos, where the apostle John wrote Revelation while imprisoned there. Overall, it gave me a good feeling. Then we spent time on the island of Rhodes, taking the steep, windy climb up top to ancient ruins. The Colossus of Rhodes, 280 BC, was a colossal statue of the Greek sun god Helios that stood in the ancient Greek city of Rhodes and was one of the Seven Wonders of the World. The statue was 110 feet tall atop a fifty-foot platform. The statue was destroyed by an earthquake in 226 BC. The west coast of Rhodes is the Aegean Sea, and the east coast is the Mediterranean. On the southern tip of the island, the seas are only separated by a narrow sandbar. Northwest winds thunder ashore from the Aegean, while the Mediterranean side can be as calm as a millpond. Then we spent a little time on the island of Mikonos, Aristotle Onassis's favorite island. Very small, not much to it. In all, it was a very pleasant journey. I completed several paintings from that trip.

Hittite Empire

The Hittites were an ancient group of Indo-Europeans who moved into Asia Minor and formed an empire at Hattusa in Anatolia (Turkey) around 1600 BC. The Hittite Empire reached great heights in the mid-1300 BC, when it spread across Asia Minor into the northern Levant and Upper Mesopotamia.

The Hittite society was feudal and agrarian, the common people being either freemen, *artisans*, or slaves. Anatolia was rich in metals, especially silver and iron. The Hittites developed iron-working technology, helping to initiate the Iron Age. Eventually, the Assyrians dominated the area and annexed most of the Hittite Empire. Nothing new under the sun.

The Bible says the Hittites were descendants of Ham, one of Noah's sons. King David had Bathsheba's husband, Uriah, killed. Uriah was a Hittite.

Babylon

Babylon, located about fifty miles south of modern Baghdad in Iraq, was an ancient city with a history of settlements dating back to the end of the third millennium BC. Established and ended: circa 1894–1595 BC. Duration: three hundred years. Founding country: Central-Southern Mesopotamia (modern-day Iraq). Babylon was a minor town in the region of Syria. Eventually, Babylon grew, and their power reached its peak under the reign of Hammurabi (circa 1728–1686 BC). After the death of Hammurabi, the Babylonian Empire began to rapidly decline, thus ending the first Babylonian empire. Under king Muršili, the Hittites sacked the capital city.

Slaves brought from foreign countries as spoils of war were mostly the children of former slaves. There were laws that involved the institution of slavery, protecting the rights of the owners, some protecting slaves. The law made it clear that even though the slave was property, the master could not maim, beat, injure, or kill them. The laws protected slaves in some ways; nevertheless, they were slaves to a master.

The Hanging Gardens of Babylon were one of the Seven Wonders of the Ancient World. The fabled gardens adorned the capital of the Neo-Babylonian Empire, built by its greatest king Nebuchadnezzar II, 605–562 BCE.

Scholars claim the gardens were actually at Nineveh, capital of the Assyrian Empire. The exotic nature of the gardens compared to the more familiar Greek items and the mystery surrounding their location and disappearance have made the Hanging Gardens of Babylon the most captivating of all the seven wonders.

The empire was founded by Nebuchadnezzar's father after his victory over the Assyrian Empire. Nebuchadnezzar II would go on to even greater things, including the capture of Jerusalem in 597 BC. The biblical account of this king is one of the most riveting narratives in the Bible. Why was Nebuchadnezzar's mind taken, and he ate grass like an ox for seven years? (Daniel 4:25–35). Babylon's origin goes back to Babel in Genesis 11, Isaiah 21:1–10, Jeremiah 50–51. Why is America called Babylon the Great in Bible prophecy? This is another interesting study. The comparison is there.

Assyrian Empire

Established and ended: circa 2025–605 BC. Duration: 1,420 years. Founding countries: parts of Iraq, Turkey, Syria, and Iran. The Assyrians were one of the major people to live in Mesopotamia during ancient times. The Assyrian Empire rose and fell several times throughout history. They did not rise to power until after the fall of the Akkadian Empire. During the height of the Assyrian Empire, it ruled over what the ancient Mesopotamian religion called the "four corners of the world." In their view, the four regions were Subartu (Assyria) in the north, Martu (Syria) in the west, Elam in the east, and Sumer in the south.

The Assyrian Empire had different forms of slaves, debt slaves, or prisoners of war. These were the lowest on the ladder of social status. The less obedient the prisoners of war were forced to become people of restricted freedom and to work in the temple or palaces. Ancient Assyrians had practical inventions, like locks and keys, paved roads, plumbing, flushing toilets, the sexagesimal clock (the way we tell time today). The Assyrians were also first to use the potter's wheel; irrigation; bronze metal, iron, and looms to weave cloth from wool; and developed glasswork and glaze. Among the great mathematical inventions were the division of the circle into 360 degrees and first to invent longitude and latitude. They also developed a sophisticated medical science as far away as Greece.

The Assyrian Empire lasted 1,420 years before being destroyed by a coalition led by Babylonians, Medes, Persians, and others, who then divided the region between them. Greedy men reaping the spoils of war. Nothing new under the sun. The area was sparsely populated thereafter, the ancient ruins slowly became buried in earth. The regions subject to Assyrian rule had been trying to break free for years and finally saw their chance. The Assyrians and their army were respected and feared—most of all, hated. By the last quarter of the seventh century BC, nearly every part of the empire was in a state of rebellion, not struggles for freedom but wars of revenge. In 612 BC, the city of Nineveh was sacked and burned by the allied forces. America's army is respected and feared and also hated by many. Pray that America doesn't end as the Assyrians did. "There is nothing new under the sun."

Nineveh

Nineveh of the Bible was an ancient city of Upper Mesopotamia, located on the outskirts of Mosul in modern-day northern Iraq. In the Bible, Nineveh represents the place God calls us not to go. Anywhere that looks like trouble or danger, Nineveh represents the places we fear. As perverse and immoral as Nineveh was, it is remembered for the people's desire for God's compassion (Jonah 4:11). This is where Jonah was sent, rebelled, was in the belly of a whale for three days, and finally preached and saw Nineveh repent.

The story of Nineveh fits America's decline perfectly. We have fallen away from God and His provisions for us. Pray for God's compassion on America and her people. Pray also for the people who hate us. "There is nothing new under the sun."

The Akkadian Empire

The second empire of ancient Mesopotamia, after the long-lived civilization of Sumer, oldest empire in the world, was established around 4,300 years ago (2278 BC). Under the empire, Akkadians and the Sumerians were united, and people were bilingual. There were eight kings over this area. Conquer and defeat! In ancient Sumer, kings would send bands of men out to plunder neighboring city-states in the hill country in order to acquire slaves. The kings would claim that their god had given them victory over inferior people.

Beware, oligarchs! Playing God is a dangerous game. God hasn't died and put you in charge. We need to know that slavery was a huge part of civilization and how the ancient near east lived. Slaves built their empires, and slaves will do it again if the Lord doesn't come soon. Do you truly get the picture? Akkad, ancient region in what is now central Iraq, was the northern division of ancient Babylonia. Located in the areas where the Tigris and Euphrates rivers are closest to each other, their Semitic language, known as Akkadian, became a literary language system of writing with the cuneiform system as the oldest Semitic dialect still preserved.

Sumer

Sumer was an ancient civilization founded in the Southern Mesopotamia region of the Fertile Crescent situated between the Tigris and Euphrates Rivers. Known for their innovations in language, government, architecture, and more, the Sumerians are considered the creators of civilization as modern humans understand it. Control of the region lasted two thousand years before the Babylonians took charge in 2004 BC.

For centuries, men have challenged the authenticity of the Bible as lack of proof for the existence of the city of Ur. The Lord said to Abram, "Leave your country, your people and your father's household and go to the land I will show you." Abram left the city-state of Ur (Genesis 12).

The Sumerian people are mentioned in the Bible. The story of the Good Samaritan. When Jesus talks with the Samaritan woman at Jacob's well (John 4:4–26).

The very first recorded true city, Uruk (Ur), at its peak population, was between forty thousand and eighty thousand people living in six miles of defensive walls, making it a contender for the largest city in the world at that time. The patron god was Nanna, the moon god, and the city's name means "the abode of Nanna." British archaeologists unearthed the ancient city of Ur right after WWI. Bible believers jumped for joy. Unbelievers had used the nonexistence of Ur as proof the Bible was in error. God's Word is a mountain of information, especially ancient histories.

Recorded evidence in Sumer culture comprised a mixture of debt slavery, slavery as a punishment for crime, and the enslavement of prisoners of war. Slavery did exist during and before biblical times. Actually, slavery existed as far back as the beginning of recorded history.

Use your brains, people. Can you not see that America's role in slavery is merely a drop in the bucket in the overall picture of slavery's evil past. Think of all the enslaved families in our country blessed to rise above their troubled past. They became respectable human beings working toward a better future; not possible back in Africa. African chiefs sold their own people into slavery, and evil men today sell out the blind, naive black people doing their bidding for them. There is nothing new under the sun.

Tamerlane

Timur (meaning *iron*) was born in 1336 AD near the city of Kesh in Transoxiana. This historic Persian city is now known as Shahrisabz in modern-day Uzbekistan. Timur was a fourteenth-century Turko-Mongol military leader who conquered most of the Muslim world, Central Asia, and parts of India. He turned his army toward India and slaughtered the Pakistani and Indian people, justifying the barbarism as a holy war against the Hindu religion.

It should be evident that evil people will do or say anything to promote their own agenda. Sound familiar? Worst of all is using religion to justify evil. Listen up! This horrible event is worth noting. The Sultan of Delhi used war elephants covered with chain mail to terrify Timur's troops. In a stroke of cruel genius, Timur placed hay on the backs of camels, set the hay afire, and prodded them until they painfully charged at the elephants. The elephants turned and stampeded their own troops, granting Timur an easy victory. The population of Delhi was massacred. This shows absolutely no respect for God, man, or beast. Personally, I don't want to live in a world like that.

Timur's cruelty grew in his later years. After destroying Delhi, he turned west. Legend states that during his invasion of Baghdad (Iraq) in 1399 required each of his soldier to show him two severed heads from the Christian population. Next and in revenge for insulting letters sent by the Ottoman sultan Bayezid (Turkey), Timur conquered the Ottoman Empire in 1402 and placed the sultan in a cage, where he eventually died in captivity.

The cruelty toward elephants and camels was also a grave sin in the eyes of God. The animal kingdom was not created to be abused by humans. Timur's conscience was seared, dead. Once the conscience has calloused over, there is no feeling for man or beast. All these idiots running around killing, raping, and destroying our cities apparently have no conscience to guide them. Excessive drug use is another culprit leading to lack of conscience.

During his mid-twenties, Tamerlane was crippled by injuries to his right leg and right hand. Legend states that he was shot by arrows when his band of thieves was ambushed by a shepherd. It is more likely the injuries were sustained in battle. The 1941 Russian excavation revealed that he was tall for the time, broad chested, had prominent cheek bones, and had Mongoloid features. On his tomb was inscribed, "When I rise from the dead, the world shall tremble." Isn't this absurd? This narcissistic maniac was nothing more than a self-centered murderous butcher, a *worm*.

Tamerlane idolized Genghis Khan and used similar methods to build his empire. Timur married a descendent of Genghis Kahn. Timur was an evil military mastermind who led a multiethnic army. His bloody reputation precedes him. He is remembered for his gruesome military campaigns in which tens of millions of people were slaughtered. He was a savage emperor, who treated human life with the same respect he would an ant. His military conquered thirteen lands.

In his youth, he led a band of petty thieves who stole livestock from farmers and property from travelers and merchants. What a pompous, puffed-up little thug. It is estimated his armies killed seventeen million people, which was about 5 percent of the global population at that time. Tamerlane's ambition was to rebuild the empire of Genghis Khan, who had died a century earlier. He referred to himself as the "sword of Islam" and converted much of his empire to the religion. This included Genghis Khan's descendants, the Borjigin clan. The Barlas tribe had converted to Islam and spoke Turkish.

The willful slaughter of human beings has always been about control. There is more than one way to eradicate a society. When unchecked, evil seeks world dominance; limitless ambition has no conscience. It is a fact that the coronavirus came from a lab in China and was deliberately spread throughout the entire world. It is obvious to me that our government is not only aware of this but willingly scatter infected migrants throughout our country. Every scripted word President Biden utters, he often bumbles. I do not trust the government to have my best interest in anything. If the crisis at our border hasn't opened your eyes and mind, then wake up! rest assured, America is on the hit list.

In 1383, Persia found itself on Timur's hit list. He plundered the ancient city of Herat of its treasures and destroyed important landmarks. Sound familiar? The Isfahan people rose up against Timur's high taxation. Sound familiar? Timur responded by slaughtering the people and building towers out of their skulls. The artisans and craftspeople were spared so they could work building his imperial capital. The city was to be the heart of the Islamic world.

The American people are witnessing dark, nefarious methods by the jerks attempting to destroy our country. They are burning our statues. Who knows what future absurdities are in store for America and her people? How do you feel about Islam now? How do you feel now about Biden's presidency? Clean up the *swamp*. Vote.

Unlike Genghis Khan's father, Tamerlane's father was a prominent member of the Barlas tribe, which had been close with Genghis Khan's Borjigin clan. Tamerlane's own religious affiliation is unclear, and he probably used Islam as a means to consolidate and exert power. He was a highly intelligent politician who spoke Turkish, Mongolian, and Persian. These tactics are "nothing new under the sun."

Tamerlane lived and died an evil man on the seventeenth of February 1405 at the age of sixty-eight. He will surely burn in hell for eternity. Don't let anyone tell you life on earth is the end. How could that ever be just? The Timurid dynasty finally ended defeated by the British Empire following the 1857 rebellion.

Genghis Khan

Genghis Kahn, 1162–1227. He established the largest land empire in history. He was born near the border between Mongolia and Siberia. His father had kidnaped his mother and forced her into marriage. Before age ten, his father was poisoned to death by an enemy clan. Temujin (Genghis Khan) was left in a violent and unpredictable world amid dozens of nomadic tribes constantly fighting and stealing from each other.

Temujin's own clan then deserted him, his mother, and his six siblings in order to avoid having to feed them.

Shortly thereafter, he killed his older half brother and took over as the leader of the clan. A poor, illiterate boy rose to be a leader of the disunited Mongols. At one point, he was captured and enslaved by the clan that had abandoned him, but he eventually escaped.

Terror was the Mongols' weapon and is applied ruthlessly. Temujin executed the leaders of enemy tribes, looted the treasury, enslaved wives and children, and the remaining people were taken into slavery by his clan. When a community was sacked and everyone slaughtered by slit throats, the remaining were led out twenty by twenty to drown in a trough of blood. It is horrible to think that humanity could stoop to such vicious, despicable behavior. Could mind-altering drugs have existed in those days?

By 1205, he had vanquished all rivals, including killing his best friend. The following year, he was proclaimed Chinggis (Genghis) Khan, which means "universal ruler." He eventually ruled over one million people. In order to suppress the traditional causes of tribal warfare, he abolished inherited aristocratic titles. He also forbade the selling and kidnapping of women, banned the enslavement of any Mongol, made livestock theft punishable by death, ordered the adoption of a writing system and a census, granted diplomatic immunity to foreign ambassadors, allowed freedom of religion well before that idea caught on elsewhere, abolished torture, encouraged trade, and created the first postal system. Genghis Khan left behind no palaces, no writings, no philosophy—nothing but territories that owed allegiances to him.

Despite the positives, Genghis Khan was responsible for the deaths of forty million people during the Mongol conquests. Since he had been a slave in his teen years, he outlawed slavery. Was he a bloodthirsty heathen or a fair and just statesman? Of course, he was a bloodthirsty heathen. People need to realize that we are only a heartbeat away from bloodthirsty heathens ready to demolish our country at all costs. History has shown that those out beating the drums for change today may be left floating in the bloody remains of society. Genghis asked to be buried in a secret place, and in the eight hundred years since his death, no one has found his tomb.

By comparison, Tamerlane almost makes Genghis Kahn look like a real powder puff. Both men will burn equally in hell for eternity. There will be justice.

Ottoman Empire

The Ottoman Empire controlled much of Southeastern Europe, Western Asia, and North Africa between the fourteenth and early twentieth centuries. Founded at the end of the thirteenth century in Northwestern Anatolia by the Turkoman tribal leader Osman I, its capital is Constantinople, founded in 1299. The empire dissolved in 1923. This Islamic superpower is the mightiest and longest lasting dynasty in world history: more than six hundred years. A superpower that went around conquering other nations and peoples, especially Christians, the Ottomans fought on the side of the Germans in WWI. However, not all the German government accepted the alliance.

The Ottomans were known for their achievements in art, science, and medicine. They excelled in calligraphy, painting, poetry, textiles and carpet weaving, ceramics, and music. The Ottomans practiced advanced mathematics, astronomy, philosophy, physics, geography, and chemistry. They invented surgical instruments still used today, such as forceps, catheters, scalpels, pincers, and lancet.

Fratricide

Under Sultan Selim, 1470, a new policy emerged, which included fratricide or the murder of brothers. Now the barbaric side is about to emerge in the midst of all those achievements. They were a brutal nation. When a new sultan is crowned, his brothers would be imprisoned. When the sultan's first son was born, his brothers and their sons would be killed. This system insured that the rightful heir would take the throne. They had children by different wives, so how else to solve the problem?

Not every sultan followed this harsh ritual. Over time, the practice evolved. In later years, the brothers would only be put in prison, not killed. Is this not horrible? It's a bloody curse, a bloody religion. How could a father do this to his own sons?

The Ottoman sacked cities as they roared across the continent, especially towns inhabited by Christians. Mankind's insatiable hunger for power has no conscience and still holds true today. Money and power still rule the roost. The threat of assassination was always a concern for a sultan; he relocated in a different place every night as a safety measure. Hopefully, he was plagued with guilt and fear; sin will do that to you

In the fourteenth century, the devshirme system was created. The devshirme came up out of the kul system of slavery that developed in the early centuries of the Ottoman Empire. The kuls were mostly prisoners from war, hostages, or slaves purchased by the state. The devshirme system required conquered Christians to give up 20 percent of their male children to the state.

Listen up, reader! Indoctrinating our children has been front and center for years and flourishing today in our schools among other public outlets, media, etc. Children were forced to convert to Islam and become slaves. Isn't that a pretty picture, all those misinformed who think Islam is a peaceful religion? Although they served as slaves, some of the converts became powerful and wealthy. Many were trained for government service or for the military. The elite military group known as the janissaries was primarily made up of forced Christian converts. This system lasted to the end of the seventeenth century.

Armenian Genocide

The kingdom of Armenia is one of the oldest countries in the world with a recorded history of about 3,500 years. (Isaiah 46:1; Jeremiah 50:20, 51:33–44). Armenia was the first state to adopt Christianity as its official religion under the rule of King Tiridates III of the Arsacid dynasty in the early fourth century.

The Armenian genocide was the most controversial and damning event associated with the Ottomans. In 1915, Turkish leaders planned to massacre Armenians living in the Ottoman Empire. Most scholars believe that about 1.5 million Armenians were killed. For years, the Turkish government has denied responsibility for the genocide. In fact, it's illegal, even today, to talk about the Armenian genocide in Turkey. At the time, my dad was fifteen years old. Think about that, both my Christian parents were alive, safe, and sound in America during the Armenian genocide. Scary to realize that powerful men will succumb to any form of evil in their quest of control.!

Suleiman the Magnificent

There is a great series about Suleiman and Harem. Roxanna (1505–1558) was born in Ruthenia western Ukraine, and she died in Constantinople, which is now Istanbul. Her father was an orthodox priest. She was taken prisoner at age twelve and sent to Topkapi Palace in Istanbul to be educated and trained according to palace etiquette. She converted to Islam and was given the name *Hurrem*, which means "the cheerful one." She was a pretty, fair-skinned young girl with light-colored hair. She surely stood out with those looks.

What made her famous was her intelligence and smiling face. Suleiman fell madly in love with her, and she eventually became his only legal wife. Hurrem insisted she must first be liberated from slavery before marriage. When the sultan agreed to Hurrem's terms, an Ottoman sultan married a haseki for the first time in history. Haseki means one belonging exclusively to the sultan. Their first son was born a year later then followed by three more sons and one daughter. Mehmed, the first son, was Suleiman's favorite child. He died at a very early age from contracting the plague. In the memory of his son, Suleiman built the Şehzade Mosque in Istanbul.

Evil is at work here. The pasha was a government official. Pasha persuaded Mustafa (a son) to assemble his army and join his father's army. At the same time, he warned Suleiman and persuaded him that Mustafa was coming to kill him. Suleiman saw this as a threat and ordered the execution of his son. The people blamed Suleiman's wife Hurrem and even the sultan himself. Who knows? I do! Hurrem's Christian upbringing flew out the window of greed. Hurrem's son would then be nominated as successor to the throne. Mustafa had three sons and two daughters. Suleiman had six sons, and Hurrem knew if Mustafa were out of the picture, then her son Selim II would inherit the throne. Cihangir, Hurrem's youngest child, died of grief shortly after news of his half brother's murder.

What we deem as a tragedy must not mean the same to these hard-hearted people who have no concept of Christian love and loyalty. Islam is warming up today for world dominance. If this happens, then by a miracle, it will be short lived.

Through Hurrem's influence on the sultan and her proficiency in palace intrigue, she wielded considerable power. Until that time, all Ottoman sons left for their districts as governors with their mothers, as was the custom. Wonder why? Hurrem was the first mother not to leave with her son because Suleiman wanted to keep her close. They wrote beautiful love letters to each other when he was away. When the other wife left the palace with her son, Hurrem became the sole female power in the palace. When the sultan was away, Hurrem oversaw all the palace business. She also worked as an intelligence officer for the sultan when he was away. Many of Istanbul's famous sites are credited to Hurrem. Hurrem died in 1558 and was buried in the courtyard of the Suleymaniye Mosque. It is said that Suleiman was so sad that he was unable to enjoy life ever again after his wife passed away.

"Throne of My Niche"

My wealth, my love,
My moonlight, My most sincere friend,
My confidant, my very existence,
My Sultana, my one and only love,
My spring, my daytime,
My sweetheart,
My laughing leaf.

Is this not beautiful? It amazes me that Suleiman could slaughter thousands of innocent people, and yet such beautiful words come from such a black heart.

This concludes our journey through ancient history. There are other conflicts to consider, but I only touched on the most interesting ones. My purpose is not to defend America's role in slavery because we are surely guilty. Slavery and its cruelty was an evil blot on the soul of our nation. All the ruckus today ignores the presence of slavery from the beginning of time.

Slavery has been around forever and is still alive and well today throughout the world. Our journey through ancient history is proof that slavery arrived before the onslaught of written history. Black people are not the only people to suffer slavery. Islam owned white European slaves. During Muslim Spain, the Moors controlled much of the peninsula. They imported white slaves from the eighth century until the Reconquista in the late fifteenth century. What about all the women and children of all races sold into sexual bondage by the Muslims? They would rather not talk about that. There are no perfect people.

The powers promoting BLM could care less about black people. My Black brothers are merely a convenience on the way to destroying our country. After listening to several Black conservative leaders, I am convinced the Black race will embrace America over and above all the lies thrown at them. We only know what we know.

America

Our society is crumbling from within. If we do not wake up soon, there will be no redemption for any race of people. Ancient Rome crumbled from within, and so is America. America has been the target of communism since the mid-1800s. Communism has absolutely zero conscience. Joseph Stalin ignored the Communist Manifesto and arbitrarily danced his own evil tune, murdering sixty million Russians who didn't agree with him. Does this not remind you of Russia's Putin? When societies keep their blinders on, darkness becomes a way of life. Personally, living in denial never served me well. Wise up! Repressed anger and resentments cannot survive in a healthy mind.

America was on the declining end of slavery, as you will learn from this brief partial journey through slave history. This is not to deny America's guilt because we certainly are guilty in a big way. Be aware that slavery was around for thousands of years before American slavery. The old herd mentality sets in—"everybody's doing it." As a young adolescent, how many times did you hear those words?

Personally, I owe reparation to no one nor do my ancestors. I grew up in the Jim Crow era, mandating racial segregation in all public facilities. As a child of Christian parents, I was taught that prejudice was wrong. I lived by that rule. No one in my family has ever owned slaves. I wasn't alive hundreds of years ago nor lived in any foreign countries supporting slavery. What gives anyone the right to pass judgment on the color of my skin or anyone else? I refuse to be intimated. Two wrongs will never make a right. What we owe is respect for all people because all people are created in the image of God. ALL lives matter! This is my family's staunch belief, and I'm sticking to it.

CHAPTER 22

The Reconquista

The Reconquista in medieval Spain was a series of campaigns by so-called Christian states to recapture territory from the Muslim Moors, who occupied a majority of the Iberian Peninsula in the early eighth century.

People are led to believe slavery was always racial, only black. It was religion and ethnicity, as much as race, which determined who became slaves. The Atlantic slave trade brought about ten to twelve million black African slaves to America. But between 1500 to 1650, when trans-Atlantic slaving was still in its infancy, more white Christian slaves were taken to Barbary than black African slaves to the Americas. Let this soak in.

Pirates (called corsair) along the Barbary Coast in North Africa would raid ships in the Mediterranean. They devastated seaside villages, capturing men, women, and children. France, England, and Spain lost thousands of ships. Villages along the coast were almost completely abandoned. There is no denying the Muslim slave trade was very real. England lost at least four hundred sailors a year to the slave trade. From 1718 to 1795, American sailors were enslaved by the Algerians in the Mediterranean and Atlantic slave trade. Replacing slaves was an ongoing course to keep up with the slave trade. (Excerpts from Robert Davis writings)

Attention must be called to the evil empires and to the men who founded them at the cost of multimillion lives. Why do societies call these murderous tyrants great men? I say they are little ass-kissing losers out to cover their own spin. Think about it! The kindest words I have are "evil, narcissistic scumbags. People will sell out to anyone any lie or anything that will promise them personal peace and affluence. There was never any guarantee. When greed sets in, the sky is the limit. These people will sell out to the highest bidder. They are cursed with a perpetual, ignorant, blind, and selfish attitude that has plagued all humanity since the "fall of man." It's all about me, myself and I.

President Abraham Lincoln, a Republican, issued the preliminary Emancipation Proclamation, declaring that as of January 1, 1863, "all persons held as slaves within the United State, or designate part of a State, the people whereof shall be in rebellion against the United States shall be then, thenceforward, and forever free."

Martin Luther King

Now these ignorant bums are trying to tear down Lincoln's statue, the man who abolished slavery when no one else would. Since then, America's African population have striven for success through demanding work, determination, and belief in God. It was the Reverend Dr. Martin Luther King Jr. who opened the doors of freedom. Unfortunately, Dr. King's message of peace is ignored by present-day liberal black leaders. These forces will consistently stir the fires of slavery and hatred to promote their own selfish agenda.

Yesterday's slavery is history; leave it there. The mind will put it to rest if given the chance. This is not exactly true of everyone because evil people will always live among us until the day a godly freedom takes charge. This includes all races; no one is perfect. Regardless of your color, whining is just another way the mind expresses anger and serves only one purpose: to drag you down into a self-centered pity party. All the reparation in the world will never change the reality of the past. Get over it! The mind will die in the devil's playpen until we cease to play his games. Never forget: the battle is for the mind, where everything is stored. Change the heart, the mind will follow.

Ancient Cultures

Ancient cultures have long histories of slavery going back to before biblical days. Western slavery goes back ten thousand years to Mesopotamia, today's Iraq, where a male slave was worth an orchard of date palms. Female slaves called on for sexual services, gaining freedom only when their master died. African chiefs sold their own people into slavery to Portuguese sailors for mere trinkets. Many slaves were kidnapped. Prince Infante D. Henrique began selling African slaves in Lagos around 1444 to 1455—called Henrique Square—where the African slave trade took root in Europe.

Several years ago, I was privileged to travel with my friend Iris through lovely Portugal. Shadows of Portugal's dark, ugly past sometimes clouded our vision. Despite this, I completed several oil paintings of Portugal's countryside.

CHAPTER 23

The Spanish Inquisition

The Spanish Inquisition was established in 1478 by Catholic monarchs Ferdinand II of Aragon and Isabella I of Castile and disbanded in 1834. Joseph Bonaparte, king of Naples, Napoleon's brother, led in the destruction of the Inquisition. The Inquisition was established to function as a tribunal identifying heretics and bringing them to justice—*their* justice and not Holy God's. The purpose was to purify the church. What a joke? Like God couldn't manage the problem. People will not truly accept any belief that is not in the heart, some even to the point of death. Catholicism has yet to clean house.

Jews who did not renounce their faith were killed or expelled from Spain. The Jews were a threat to the monarchy. The monarchy feared a popular uprising, and the expulsion of the Jews would end the problem—also the acquisition of their property after they were gone. Jews and Muslims fled the country in droves. At least a million people were killed during the Inquisition, murdered by Roman Catholic Spaniards. These murderers could never, ever call themselves Christians at any time. The pogroms of 1391 were especially brutal, and the threat of violence hung heavy over the Jewish community in Spain.

Pogroms

The Slavic language's term originally entered the English language to describe nineteenth- and twentieth-century violent attacks on Jews in the Russian Empire. A pogrom is a violent riot aimed at the massacre or expulsion of an ethnic or religious group. We certainly see organized violent riots in America under the umbrella of racism and reparations demanding justice. All lies!

The history of Jews in Russia and areas historically connected with it goes back at least 1,500 years. Jews in Russia have historically constituted a large religious and ethnic diaspora. The Russian Empire at one time hosted the largest population of Jews in the world: Ashkenazi Jews. Russian pogroms, while massacring Jews, brought destruction and devastation of towns and country. The communist-inspired Antifa and BLM aimed at the destruction of our cities while running around, screaming for reparations. Nothing new. These evil intentions cost the lives of billions throughout history.

The first extreme pogroms followed the assassination of Tsar Alexander II and his entire family in 1881. Only one Jew was associated with him, but false rumors aroused

Russian mobs in more than two hundred cities and towns to attack Jews and destroy their property. In the two decades following, the pogroms became less prevalent, but from 1903 to 1906, they were common throughout Russia.

How can people be so naive and still breathe? Once our nation is burned to the ground by mob rule or maybe God's vengeance against evil, then what? You may not be around to answer that question. The year 1881 was a long time ago. Basic evil instincts never change. This serves to prove my point. Nothing new under the sun. We only know what we know.

Few people know Peter the Great's core beliefs. Russia remained unaffected by the liberalizing tendencies of this era with respect to the status of Jews. Before the eighteenth century, Russia maintained an exclusionary policy toward Jews in accordance with the anti-Jewish precepts of the Russian Orthodox Church. When asked about admitting Jews into the empire, Peter the Great stated, "I prefer to see in our midst nations professing Mohammedanism and paganism rather than Jews. They are rogues and cheats. It is my endeavor to eradicate evil, not to multiply it." Peter the Great was a worm.

Slavery remained a major institution in Russia until 1723, when Peter the Great converted the household slaves into house serfs. As an indication of the extent of the slavery system in 1712, there is hardly a Cossack in Yakutsk who does not have slaves. The 2018 Global Slavery Index estimated 794,000 people currently living in a state of slavery-like conditions in Russia. This includes forced labor, forced prostitution, debt bondage, forced servile marriages, exploitation of children, and forced prison labor. These atrocities leave no corner of the globe untouched. Perverts all stem from the same universal evil pool—greedy men. These hardened hearts must surely deny the existence of the holy God.

A brief history of Peter the Great is befitting here. Peter was born on June 9, 1672 in Moscow, Russia. He was named after the Apostle Peter. What a pity he didn't follow after his namesake. Peter was the fourteenth child of Czar Alexis by his second wife. Having ruled jointly with his brother Ivan V from 1682, when Ivan died in 1696, Peter was officially declared sovereign of all Russia. In 1718, Peter the Great had his eldest son tortured to death for allegedly conspiring against him. This is beyond horrible. Apparently, Peter had zero respect for the mother either. Power hungry *worms* throughout humanity have no conscience or respect for human life other than their own. There is nothing new under the sun.

While in Saint Petersburg, we toured the beautiful, magnificent Winter Palace, the main residence of the Russian tsars. The Winter Place is also known as The Hermitage Museum. I missed many famous paintings as the crowds were packed liked sardines. We couldn't even walk. Another visit to the Kremlin Armoury proved to be a wonderful experience.

The armory is home to the Russian Diamond Fund. It houses a unique collection of art from the fifth to the twentieth century. One of the highlights was the imperial crown of Russia, the ivory throne of Ivan the Terrible, and other regal thrones and regalia: the Orlov diamond, famous Fabergé eggs, beautiful jewelry, and a collection of beautiful carriages. Another floor housed Peter the Great's ceremonial robe, his huge high boots and cane (Peter was six foot seven), the exotic gold and turquoise throne given to Boris Godunov, and many beautiful crowns—one was a gift from the Byzantine emperor Constantine, used to crown all the tsars up to 1682.

Peter's successor was Catherine the Great. As a child, Catherine didn't speak the language, married the wrong man, and then decided to change the country. Derided both in her day and modern times as a hypocritical war-monger with an unnatural sexual appetite, Catherine was a woman of contradictions whose brazen exploits have long overshadowed the accomplishments that won her "the Great." Traveling through Russia with my sister Frances, we toured Catherine's beautiful castle.

The oligarchs calling the shots in our country are not above the same exploits as Peter the Great. They could care less about the BLM idiots raging through American cities. These poor, misinformed people are nothing more than pawns on the world stage. When no longer useful, they will end up on the dump heaps of society along with the middle class. Don't look for reparations; not going to hap-pen. These monsters might give you all the barbwire you could eat. More than a hundred million people have been slaughtered just during our brief journey through history. Don't believe for a second any of us—black, white, yellow, or red—are above discrimination.

Charlie Manson

Vulnerable people are open season for cult leaders or anyone gifted with seductive words aimed at gullible, often needy individuals in search of acceptance and provision. One such case is the Charles Manson cult. He was born to Kathleen Maddox, a sixteen-year-old girl who was both an alcoholic and a prostitute. Charlie was the product of a very short marriage to William Manson. He was placed in a boy's school at age twelve. Kathleen was imprisoned for robbery. Charlie then moved in with his aunt's family, where he caused nothing but trouble from the outset. He lied constantly, always blamed others for anything he did that was wrong. He was so determined to be the center of attention that he'd deliberately misbehave while grownups were around. He displayed violet tendencies from early childhood.

Charlie became a master manipulator of people. In first grade he recruited gullible classmates, mostly girls, to attack other students that he didn't like. He was never held responsible for his actions. Charlie usually got off scot-free, while his disciples were punished. He was capable of violent outbreaks himself. His cousin said, once you got to know Charlie, nothing he did was a surprise. Rejection was entrenched in Charlie's psyche from birth, causing him to desperately seek for acceptance or just to be noticed, a very sad situation that homeless children contend with today.

Only God knows what awful things may have happened to Charlie from birth until his mother's incarceration. His biological father may have had mental problems;

he is never mentioned. Charlie just wanted his revenge. I don't believe Charlie ever knew his father. Parental separation will affect a child's development.

What baffles me is how reasonably sane people could fall for Charlie's manipulation and then commit murders for him. Ask the same question of today's youth. How can a well-read, reasonably sane person believe evil intent, then blindly follow the destruction of a perfectly functional business? A family's livelihood means absolutely nothing to these week-minded fools. Yes, there is something terribly wrong with people who allow nefarious leaders to influence their destructive behavior, including murder. I would like to believe it is only the drug culture, but it's doubtful. Drugs cause reasonable people to do unreasonable things. It certainly makes sense that Charlie Manson and his entire clan were on powerful drugs. God help us!

Popes

Evil is not limited to the drug culture. Powerful men of old, from all levels of society, fell prey to malicious intent. Perhaps drug use was practiced in ancient cultures. I don't know. It doesn't take drugs to insight an evil mind. A perfect example is Pope Sixtus IV, a flaming homosexual, whose nephew was his lover. He had a romping sex life, including six illegitimate children, whom he provided for with papal money. This man established taxes on prostitution and penalized priests and cardinals for having mistresses. This pope signed the papal bull that authorized the

Spanish Inquisition. Pope Sixtus IV was nothing more than a self-centered, self-gratifying pervert. This entire era was another evil blot on Catholicism and on humanity itself. This account only partially touches the horrible truths haunting Catholicism's despotic rule.

Pope John Paul was a breath of fresh air among centuries of popes. Pope John Paul, 1978–2005, apologized for millennia of grievous violence and persecution from the Inquisition to a wide range of sins against Jews, nonbelievers, and the indigenous people of colonized lands. He repented for the errors of his church over the previous two thousand years. In my opinion, Pope John Paul II was the first and only good pope in the history of the Roman Catholic Church. This pope in power today is a flaming communist leading his flock astray. His sins will not be overlooked.

Here is another Roman Catholic *chiller*. Pope Nicholas V, in 1452, authorized Alfonso V of Portugal to conquer Saracens (Muslims) and pagans then consign them to perpetual servitude. This Pope gave permission to continue the slave trade in West Africa under the provision that all people enslaved convert to Christianity. An impossible demand, as true conversion comes only from the heart. This pope wasn't ignorant; his purpose was evil. It is impossible for me to ever embrace Catholicism, not only for past sins but the structure is too legalistic, the antithesis of Jesus. Pedophilia is also a problem in the priesthood. You only know what you know.

At one time, popes married and had children. The problem arose when popes wanted their children to inherit the papacy. They even killed each other over the matter. Men are not gods.

The first two hundred kidnaped black slaves from West Africa arrived in this enclave in the heart of southern Portugal's Algarve region. The Portuguese soon expanded their trade along the whole coast of Africa. Lagos, Portugal, is where the African slave trade first took root in Europe. The slave trade had been active for centuries in the east long before Lagos came onto the scene.

The precise beginning of slavery is difficult to track because its origins predate historical recording and the written word. The practice of human slavery grew as the world became more civilized and organized. Civilized? Sumer is still thought to be the birthplace of slavery, which grew out of Sumer into Greece then into other parts of the ancient world. Hopefully, these facts of slavery have opened eyes and hearts.

Compassion is a virtue; call upon it! All the rioting in the world can never erase slavery's hideous history. You can, however, erase it from your heart and mind and turn your strengths toward becoming a better person and a productive citizen worthy of your labors. Take responsibility for the betterment of all races, not just a few. This is true reparation! Violence is never the answer for achieving anything you deem worthwhile. "Do not lean on your own understanding" (Proverbs 3:5–6).

Throughout history, mankind destroys societies and its peoples, planning to bring about change through total control: kill off the unwanted and the rebellious ones. Eventually, along comes another egotist playing god with all the answers and proceeds to sack your empire. All the raging idiots burning our cities, killing and injuring people will never find what they are seeking through these tactics. There will be a price to pay even after your death. Spreading fear works on the masses, not the few who will band together for the hope of humanity. "There is nothing new under the sun."

Personally, I'm not afraid of the devil himself. Only cowardly people are susceptible to fear tactics. If mankind had the power to fix all our problems, then why does the world only increase in evil and chaos? I don't have all the answers to solve the world's ills, but I do understand why problems exist, and I know the road to righteousness is redemption.

We should not look at man's physical body or his bank account but see his inner spirit. Open your spiritual eyes if you have them. What is happening to my beloved country breaks my heart. We have seen all the valleys and peaks, heartbreak and joy, failures and successes. Politicians rise and fall. All these things are the substance we derive from.

Our world is not perfect nor the people in it. Capitalism is far from perfect, but our constitutional freedoms are unsurpassed be any other system of government. It *abolished* slavery! We built a country, set people free from poverty, and provided opportunity for home ownership. If we live long enough, we reap what we sow, failure or success. Without a doubt, all this chaos, killings, and destructive behavior will one day come back to haunt these fools, including all the uninformed idiots who voted against our freedoms in the last election.

I do forgive our clueless tax-paying citizens for their ignorance and those who voted their feelings rather than their brains. Feelings are unreliable. Someday, righteousness will come down hard on the powers that fan the flames of hatred and sold out our country and its people for the almighty dollar. This world is in for a rude awaking. Our bodies will respond to the way we think. Your brains will always suck up what you put in it. Think about that!

We now have several mogul billionaires using a portion of their fortunes to bring down America and control the world and all the people in it via the New World Order. These greedy, evil worms will sit atop the heap, using their fortunes to rule all the little people. The bigger they are, the harder they fall. I'll not lose any sleep over it. People should know these powerful men are the problem and not part of the solution. Don't fall victim to their lies. Imagine this: my generation is in the way. We tell the truth! All those fools destroying our cities, paid for by the rich man's droppings, have no intelligent answers; don't care. Some people fight just to fight. They are like a herd running at random without a herdsman, programed for yelling racism at any given reason. Hundreds of societies that came before us also thought they had all the answers. Well, think again! Promises will not be honored but ignored and forgotten. The only thing the people will reap are the weeds left to wilt in the noon sun. Until the Lord returns, the poor will eventually be denigrated once again, as will everything else we love and cherish.

According to God's Word, the New World Order is inevitable. Yes, the Bible speaks of this evil intent.

Everything is in place now. Understood and embraced this prophecy for a very long time. I pray my voice will continue to expose the wickedness and warn of impending dangers that would be very foolish to ignore. This world may soon see the worst seven years of evil powers ever known to man. Considering ancient history, this says plenty.

In the past 3,421 years of recorded history, only 268 have seen no war. Only twenty-six days of peace since 1945 in America. At least 108 million people were killed during the twentieth century. Estimates for the total number killed in wars throughout human history range in the billions. It's impossible to bury these facts deep enough to have a sense of false security. What did all this accomplish other than more of the same? There is nothing new under the sun. While we still have a voice, wake up, stand up, and speak up. The time is now!

Since its inception, Marxists have tried to stuff communism down the throats of all humanity. Communist dialectics is two steps forward, one step backward. It's not rocket science to see a step forward is one gained in pursuit of a final destination. This requires single-minded patience!

Joseph Stalin forced his own views of socialism on his people and is responsible for the genocide of forty million Russians who disagreed with him or had no choice for one reason or another and 1.7 million in the Gulags. Joseph Stalin established the brutal Gulags during his long dictatorial reign. Prisoners were required to work up to fourteen hours a day, regardless of circumstances. People died of starvation, disease, exhaustion, or execution.

The Gulags were brutal labor camps established for economic and political purposes rather than elimination of inferior races like the concentration camps tried to achieve. Gulag camps were located mostly in remote areas of Siberia, where people also froze to death. Antiquity proves genocide a reality. Who is to say that killing social classes and political groups will never happen in America? Over half a million Americans have died so far of COVID deliberately released on the world from China. Whether you believe it or not, doesn't change the truth.

The largest number of mass murders goes to China's Chairman Mao in the twentieth century. Mao tops the charts. Now, Biden and his gang of trillionaire misfits are sucking up to China. Again, let me repeat: Biden, in his stupor, is merely a pawn soon to be discarded when no longer useful in the scheme of things. There is nothing new under the sun. Advice: stay alert and stay informed. Evil knocks!

Mao's most infamous experiment in social engineering is called the Great Leap Forward. This campaign caused the death of tens of millions and catapulted Mao Zedong into the big league of 20th-century murderers. The Great Leap Forward took place in late 1957 when Mao visited Moscow for the grand celebration of the 40th anniversary of the October Revolution. When the Soviet Union launch the world's first satellite, Sputnik,

Mao felt his accomplishments overshadowed. He returned to Beijing eager to assert China's position as the world's leading Communist nation. This along with his general impatience, spurred a series of increasingly reckless decisions that led to the worst famine in history. Later Mao pushed for the creation of communes-effectively nationalizing farmers property. Look for this to happen in our country. People were to eat in canteen and share agricultural equipment, livestock, and production with food allocated by the state. (Excerpt from a writing by Ian Johnson in 2018)

Wake up, America. I don't see our spoiled people falling into that trap, at least I pray not. We should question those who do business with this evil, inhumane regime. It is difficult to avoid buying anything made in China. Most people never give this a second thought because China's foot is firmly planted in our economy and the minds of Americans. It is time to wake up our sleeping giant once again. Start by buying only "made in America."

Socialism has only two classes of peoples, the controlling rich and the extremely poor. A mere few millions will not qualify you for the upper class; it may take billions. The middle class will just simply disappear. This is why our history is being systematically destroyed, altering our language, our choice of words, our speech, our habits, our minds—all so prevalent today. Once you have completed this book, then you should understand why it's necessary to destroy all history. Because history will expose all the lies we hear today from our government and political parties, which plans to destroy our country and our way of life. The black hand of censorship is working overtime to silence conservative voices. With only half a brain, one should be able to figure that out. The power hungry envision a world of obedient little robots all marching in a row. Anything else would be too difficult to control; even that will meet its demise.

Hopefully, the brainwashed little robots will make a concerted effort to search beyond their present mindset. Intelligence is the ability to acquire knowledge and skills. Not everyone who disagrees with you is wrong. Pigheaded people create their own tiny space in the world and never attempt to learn about or understand the opinions of others or their experiences. This kind of truth is based on a limited knowledge and understanding within their tiny space. Truth is also not relevant. Real and honest truth is absolute. Why not strive for the mind of Christ? Learn to rattle off truths faster than the mighty cheetah in pursuit of prey.

The worldview says, "Don't dare attempt to think or speak your own mind. You may be eliminated." We battle against global powers not interested in America, only in promoting communist China's desire for world dominance and to line their own pockets. Our government has failed us, including the CIA, Department of Justice, FBI, and all the rest. Sucking up to China will never be the answer.

China's eventual doom is also inevitable. Sucking up to Russia is a losing proposition. Vladimir Putin is a five-foot-seven little thug with a terrible "Napoleon complex," desperate to prove his strength at all costs.

After nearly eighty-eight years of freedom to choose, refuse, or make mistakes, the power of controlling forces will never influence my behavior or my beliefs. Amen! Nero fed praying, smiling Christians to the lions while the crowd cheered. Well, bring it on! Wake up, all you little robots; put on your big-boy pants. Ignorance is no excuse.

Embracing Christianity is a choice. How can one choose anything without understanding all the benefits or the pitfalls? Cling to the truth. Evil is very real; conforming to evil should be unacceptable for any intelligent human being. The ignorant among us are blind and without excuse, including all you geniuses. They are searching for answers in all the wrong places for all the wrong reasons. There are always two sides to everything. An intelligent person would surely set about an in-depth study of all opposing views. There is no other way to reach a rational intelligent decision. Don't depend on the "boob tube" or the opinions of liars as your source of truth. God takes care of the truly feeble. The world will never give permission to speak your mind. Might as well try a refreshing twenty-mile swim upstream in one breath.

Years ago (maybe the '60s), I watched a very dark, disturbing movie, *The Red Door*. There have been several Red Door movies since that may or may not send the same message as the original. It's doubtful. The original movie tells of a time when people were policed, confined to their homes, and forbidden to read or own books. There was one family with a large library who refused to conform and managed to hide books. Some hateful person or group protested and turned the family over to the book police. The book police confiscated the books, burning them all. The family was then punished in some way, all books thrown into a huge constantly burning bonfire.

This unsettling story left a lasting impression on my mind. Now I realize it was a warning of things to come, a foreshadow of today. Don't remember the author; he was surely a brave sole. Of course, the original is nowhere to be found. I remember thinking at the time, *This could never happen in America.* Well, people, we are there.

Another subject I want to approach with concern is the world's superpowers. The order of the day is to move everyone to a central control, including your money. Shades of *The Red Door.* Very soon, we will be a cashless society that Bible prophecy foretold thousands of years ago. Trust me, this is here. First a global economic crisis must take place, turning the populous upside down.

Is this not in progress now? Those who want to buy and sell must have a chip (mark) put on the right hand or the forehead so that no one can buy or sell unless he has the mark, that is, the mark of the beast or the number of its name 666 (Revelation 13:1–18). As long as people are using cash, transactions can be completed in private, but if all currency becomes electronic, then every transaction can be monitored.

We are monitored all the time right now, especially our speech and, when necessary, our bank accounts. There are those who deny this interpretation and make a vain attempt to change the original wording or substitution of one thing or another. They are sorely mistaken. Since we practically live in a cashless society now, Revelation's prophecy is perfectly logical. Right on target, at least you won't be surprised when this happens.

If I am alive and kicking, the chip will never enter any part of my body even to the point of death. Never will I compromise my principles for evil intent. Our present society is primed and ready for such action. We are headed to an oligarchy form of government like the English aristocratic oligarchy. I believe it's entirely possibly a group of billionaires will try to establish an oligarchy form of government. Regardless of who controls our government, our nation and our Constitution hang in the balance. If interested, there is much more to learn on this subject.

Oligarchy countries includes Russia, China, Saudi Arabia, Iran, Turkey, and England. Most formed from family dynasties. Oligarchs rule England. The United States has falsely been described as an oligarchy because economic elites and special interest groups have substantial independent impacts on US Government policy, while average citizens and mass-based interest groups have little or no independent influence. Now that Biden and his goons are in charge, we the people had better speak up, or we the people will have no voice. The ruling class plans to destroy our Constitution, our protection. My voice is not always modest, sometime lacking in substance, occasionally loud but sincerely mine.

CHAPTER 24

Faith and Science

It's a fallacy to believe that faith and science are mutually exclusive. Many people profess to believe in science. I believe scientific discoveries have greatly contributed to the advancement of humankind. To believe scientific facts and totally believe in science are two different things.

Not all scientists are atheists as you will discover in the following article:

Faith and Science: Which Is Right?
(Barry Cooper)

In the war between science and religion, which side is right?

Science and religion cannot be reconciled... Religion has failed, and its failures should stand exposed. Science should be acknowledged king [Peter Atkins].

The words of the British chemist Peter Atkins express the idea that faith and science are mortal enemies. Each threatens to swallow up the other. Only one can win.

Science—particularly evolutionary science—has made belief in God an anachronism. Religious faith is a throwback to an intellectually primitive, anti-scientific past. We once believed in God because we had nothing else to illuminate the dark places of our ignorance. But as scientific knowledge grows, God will shrink—until finally, the argument runs, he will shrivel into non-existence.

As Carl Sagan once said, "As science advances, there seems to be less and less for God to do... Whatever it is we cannot explain lately is attributed to God... And then, after a while, we explain it, and so that's no longer God's realm."

But is that true? Are science and belief really mutually exclusive? Or might there be a more complementary relationship at play?

Faith vs. Science

If scientific knowledge drives out religious faith, we would expect to find very few exemplary scientists who believe in God. But that isn't the case.

Copernicus, Kepler, Pascal, Galileo, Faraday, and Newton are some of the most celebrated scientists in history, and they were all theists. Their faith in God didn't inhibit or threaten their scientific endeavors. If anything, the reverse seems to have been true.

For example, Robert Boyle (the founder of modern chemistry) argued that the study of science would only increase our wonder at the way God had ordered his creation. Far from posing a threat to faith, then, science fueled his theistic convictions. And far from posing a threat to science, faith motivated his scientific curiosity.

More recently, there are many examples of exceptional scientists whose belief in God coexists productively with scientific endeavor. Think of Francis Collins, the former head of the Human Genome Project, Nobel Prize-winner Antony Hewish, or the prominent botanist Sir Ghillean Prance, who said, "All my studies in science...have confirmed my faith."

Stephen Jay Gould, the late Harvard scientist and evolutionist who was himself an atheist, concluded: "Either half my colleagues are enormously stupid, or else the science of Darwinism is fully compatible with conventional religious beliefs—and equally compatible with atheism."

Many believers would argue in a similar vein: science does not disprove the existence of God or his involvement in the creation and sustainment of our world—just as religious beliefs do not disprove the discoveries of science.

So it would seem that perhaps science and religious faith can be compatible entities. I want to suggest that this is the case because, for the most part, they're asking complementary rather than conflicting questions.

QUESTIONS OF MEANING AND PURPOSE

There are many questions the Bible doesn't address—questions that are wonderfully addressed by science. The Bible doesn't tell me how to make a vaccine for polio, launch a satellite into space, or put topspin on a tennis ball.

At the same time, there are many questions addressed by Jesus that are not addressed by science—nor can they ever be. That isn't a slight on science; it's just recognition that there are limits to what it can tell us. Steve Jones, the professor of genetics at University College London and an atheist, put it like this: "Science cannot answer the questions that philosophers or children ask: Why are we here? What is the point of being alive? How ought we to behave?"

Questions of meaning and purpose cannot be addressed by scientific discoveries, however magnificent.

The scientist John Lennox gives a quirky illustration of this. Imagine, he says, that Aunt Matilda has made a cake. And she has made it for a particular purpose.

Now, there are lots of things scientists could tell us about the cake. Nutrition scientists can tell us about the number of calories in the cake and its nutritional effect; biochemists can tell us about the structure of the proteins and the fats; chemists can tell us about the elements involved and their bonding; physicists can analyze the cake in terms of fundamental particles; mathematicians can give us a beautiful set of equations to describe the behavior of those particles.

But does that satisfy all our questions?

Yes, we know how the cake is put together. We know all about its constituent parts and the way they relate to each other. No higher power told us any of that; science did. But can our scientists tell us why the cake was made?

Only the maker—in this case, Aunt Matilda—knows. And until she reveals that information to us, no amount of scientific genius will be able to discover it.

QUESTIONS SCIENCE CAN'T REACH

It's one thing to listen to the maker of a cake. But imagine for a moment that there is a maker of the world. What would it be like to listen to that entity talk about why he or she made it—made us? Imagine for a moment that there is a God. We would be able to get answers—definitive answers—to our deepest questions. The questions that science can't reach.

The claim made by Jesus is exactly that. He claims to be our Maker come to earth.

The book of Hebrews in the Bible says that Jesus is "the radiance of God's glory and the exact representation of his being, sustaining all things by his powerful word." He is our Maker, visiting us in space-time history, explaining our lives to us in the way that only our Maker can.

There's no need to abandon scientific curiosity to believe in God. In fact, I would encourage you to listen to your scientific instincts and follow the evidence wherever it takes you, even if it takes you somewhere unexpected. Similarly, you don't have to give up your belief in God to explore what science has discovered about our world. Give it a try, and you may just find that the two can coexist harmoniously.

I do believe that science plays a huge part in our progress. I also know and believe that God, our Creator, leads mankind to discover the positive aspects of science. However, when mankind blatantly takes all the credit for every new and beneficial discovery, he is denying the Holy God. Science enables us to fulfill the mandate of Genesis 1:28.

CHAPTER 25

New World Order

The World Economic Forum is headed by Professor Klaus Schwab, founder and executive chairman of the World Economic Forum. He says, "Now is the time for the Great Reset" (May 25, 2022). *The Fourth Industrial Revolution* by Klaus Schwab is a shocking foretelling of things to come. His ubiquitous plans are mobile supercomputing, intelligent robots, self-driving cars, neurotechnological brain enhancements, genetic editing, etc. The evidence of dramatic change is all around us. And it's happening at exponential speed.

Schwab is a former member of the Bilderberg Group—a powerful international secret society made up of six hundred wealthy and influential individuals and has an aggressive plan to achieve world domination. Here's just a partial list of the members you might recognize: Sam Altman, Jeff Bezos, Bill Gates, H. J. Heinz (deceased), David Rockefeller, Ben Bernanke (federal reserve), Tom

Daschle, John Edwards, Chuck Hagel, John Kerry, Bill Clinton, Rick Perry, Sandy Berger, Hillary Clinton, Dick Gephardt, Lindsey Graham, Henry Kissinger, Jare Kushner, David Petraeus, Condoleezza Rice, Tony Blair, Margaret Thatcher, Angela Merkel, and Klaus Schwab to name a few.

I was first enlightened on Bilderberg's New World Order during the late 1980s—a frightening discovery. Unlike today, with the internet, there was very little information available to the public at that time. Fortunately, I knew where to search out the truth and uncover the lies.

Nineteen Shocking Facts and Theories about the Bilderberg Group ("19 Shocking Facts and Theories about the Bilderberg Group" [theclever.com])

The Bilderberg Group meets once every year. The last meeting, at the time of this writing, was held in June 2016 at the Taschenbergpalais Hotel, which is located in Dresden. Up to 150 of the world's wealthiest and most powerful political leaders attended the annual event. The attendees include royalties, presidents, prime ministers, chief executives of major international conglomerates, media moguls, and world bankers.

The first Bilderberg meeting was held during 1954. The organization was founded with the intent to create powerful connections between European countries and North Americans. The meeting was a secretive, informal discussion about global trends with open communication between the elite members of the world who have massive influence in world affairs.

No statements of any kind are allowed to be made to the press regarding the proceedings or what is talked about at the meeting. There are no meeting minutes taken, and no reports or official statements about the discussions is produced or made. Anything learned at the meeting can be freely used by any of the members; however, no one is permitted to talk about it.

More than four hundred heavily armed guards were there to protect the attendees. The event space was hardened with physical barricades and high levels of security. It was this level of high security combined with the extreme secrecy, which made the conspiracy theorists go wild with speculation about what they actually do at the Bilderberg meetings.

Only those who are invited are permitted to attend the meeting. Everyone invited sees a major career boost after attending a Bilderberg meeting. Bill Clinton attended while he was the governor of Arkansas, and within a year, he was the president of the United States. Tony Blair became prime minister of the UK four years after going to his first Bilderberg meeting.

19. Founded by an ex-Nazi and an agent of the Vatican (via the Astral News)

The cofounders of the Bilderberg Group were two historical figures with checkered backgrounds. They were Prince Bernhard from the Netherlands and Józef Retinger, who was a political advisor originally from Poland and worked with the Vatican.

Throughout his later adult life up until his death in 1984, Prince Bernhard claimed he was never a Nazi. A historian, Annejet van der Zijl, found documents at the Humboldt University in Berlin, which proved that Prince Bernhard was indeed a Nazi Party member until 1934 when he left school to work for the huge German chemical company named IG Farben. IG Farben did atrocious things in support of the Nazis, including making the poisonous gas used to kill people in the German death camps.

Józef Retinger was a secret spy for the Vatican. He was expelled from allied countries for his activities in association with the Jesuits. He later went on to create the Council of Europe during 1949, which became part of the foundational movement and eventually led to the formation of the European Union.

18. Serious conflicts of interest (via Conspiratainment)

The Bilderberg Group publishes on its website a simple list of the items that will be discussed at an upcoming meeting without giving any further details. For the 2016 meeting, here was the list of the topics up for discussion:

China, current events, cybersecurity, Europe (growth, immigrants, reform, unity and vision), geopolitics of energy and commodities, lower classes and the middle class, Middle East, Russia, technological innovation, US political climate, economy, debt, growth, and reform.

The Bilderberg Group also publishes a list of the attendees. By comparing the attendees with the proposed agenda, it is easy to see the potential conflicts of interest. A high probability must exist of shady "backroom" deals and influence peddling. Hilary Clinton always attends, and she has received millions of dollars in "speaker's fees" from other attendees.

The chairman of BP, Carl-Henric Svanberg; the group chief executive of BP, Robert Dudley; the vice-chairman of Galp Energia from Portugal; and the CEO of Royal Dutch Shell all met with finance ministers and top political leaders. After the Bilderberg Group meeting, they do not report back to their respective governments about what happened.

Other attendees of the 2016 meeting included former European commission president José Manuel Barroso; former US secretary of state Henry Kissinger; US senator Lindsey Graham; Christine Lagarde, who is the director of the International Monetary Fund; German defense minister Ursula von der Leyen; German interior minister Thomas de Maizière; German finance minister Wolfgang Schäuble; King Willem-Alexander of the Netherlands; a former head of the CIA, General David Petraeus; and a former head of MI6, Sir John Sawers.

17. The who's who of the world (via Daily Mail)

Members of the Bilderberger Group are some of the richest, most powerful, and most famous people in the world. Attendees from past Bilderberg meetings include the following:

Angela Merkel; Beatrix of the Netherlands; Bill Clinton; Bill Gates; Carl Bildt Charles; Prince of Wales; Charlie Rose; Colin Powell; Condoleezza Rice; David Cameron; Dora Bakoyannis; Enoch Powell; Fouad Ajami; Frank McKenna; Fredrik Reinfeldt; Geir Haarde; George P. Shultz; George Soros; George Stephanopoulos; Georgios Alogoskoufis; Gerald Ford; Gordon Brown; Gordon Campbell; Guido Westerwelle; Haakon, Crown Prince of Norway; Harald V of Norway; Henry Kissinger; Jeff Bezos; John Edwards; John Kerr; John Kerry; Jon Huntsman Jr.; José Manuel Barroso; Juan Carlos I of Spain; Kathleen Sebelius; Lawrence Summers; Lester B. Pearson; Margaret Thatcher; Mario Draghi; Mark Sanford; Paul Volcker; Peter Mandelson; Peter Sutherland; Prince Philip, Duke of Edinburgh; Queen Sofía of Spain; Rick Perry; Robert Zoellick; Ruud Lubbers; Sandy Berger; Timothy Geithner; Tom Daschle; and William F. Buckley Jr.

16. Conspiracy theories (via Voice of the People)

The Bilderberg Group is a conspiracy theorist's dream scenario. Since no one except the attendees of the Bilderberg meetings knows what is said or done, anything imaginable might be going on. Author David Ike says the

"Bilderbergers" are shapeshifting lizards doing the work of the Illuminati. He imagines this group as a potentially satanic cabal that controls everything that happens in the world, which has the intention of enslaving the entire human race.

Alex Jones from Infowars consistently rants on air about the evil of this group. From his point of view, everything that appears to be happening in the world from normal methods is actually the results of behind-the-scenes manipulation by members of this group. There are historical precedents for some of what he says, such as the "false flag" event at the Gulf of Tonkin that brought the USA into the war in Vietnam.

There is no question whatsoever that the members of the Bilderberg Group are extremely powerful and can do many things, especially if they coordinate their efforts.

Infowars reported that the Bilderberg Group wants to create an Internet ID and a global tax on online financial transactions and travel by air. The justification for the Internet ID is that it would improve cybersecurity, reduce fraud, and make it easier to receive government services. Critics of the plan say that the Internet ID is a virtual passport that would remove the ability to obtain Internet services anonymously. This "big brother" way to track everything a person does online will make political dissent impossible.

The plans for an Internet ID are similar to the plans to use microchips embedded in the skin as a way of personal identification. Any such plan that forces these types of technology on people is an invasion of their personal privacy. Therefore, this idea should be resisted by those who like freedom of speech and do not want information about everything they do online to be used in ways that they do not approve.

15. *Secret Bilderberg affiliations (via Stillness in the Storm)*

Paul Warburg founded the Council on Foreign Relations during 1921, and David Rockefeller founded the Trilateral Commission. These organizations are similar to the Bilderberg Group. David Rockefeller is a member of all three.

The current members of these groups and the previous ones make it easy to see how powerful they are. Members include almost all the US presidential candidates from both political parties, congresspersons, senators, and the top officials at the CIA, FBI, and the NSA. Members include the captains of industry, leaders of defense organizations, Supreme Court justices, generals, and admirals.

Just like the Bilderberg Group, the extent and reach of the powerful members of the Council on Foreign Relations and the Trilateral Commission have influenced the globe for decades.

It makes very little difference who is the president in the White House because these power brokers are the ones really in charge. In most cases, without their approval and support, there is no way to get elected.

14. *Control of the world's central banks (via Anonymous)*

Another cofounder of the Council on Foreign Relations was Edward Mandell House. He was the chief adviser to President Woodrow Wilson. Two things happened of significance by the influence of Edward Mandell House. During the December 1913 holiday season, when many of the lawmakers were not working, the Federal Reserve Act was quietly passed, which gave the power to create money to the bankers.

Following this, the Sixteenth Amendment was ratified during February 1914. This amendment created the federal income tax in order to have tax revenues to pay the debt for the money loaned to the government by the bankers. Americans have these powerful men to blame for creating the massive US debt and for US tax.

The common goal of the Council on Foreign Relations and the Bilderberg Group is the creation of a one-world government with a central global financial system. The two groups work together. The Council on Foreign Relations works on the US side with the Bilderberg Group working on the European side.

13. *Global military control (via the United Nations)*

During the 1992 Bilderberg Group meeting, Henry Kissinger said, "Today, Americans would be outraged if UN troops entered Los Angeles to restore order. Tomorrow, they will be grateful. This is especially true if they were told there was an outside threat from beyond, whether real or imagined, that threatened our very existence. It is then that all people of the world will plead with world leaders to deliver them from this evil…individual rights will be willingly relinquished for the guarantee of their well-being granted to them by their world government."

There have been many instances in history where false information has been used to start wars. One recent one was when the false threat of Saddam Hussein having weapons of mass destruction was used as the pretense for the Iraq war. One way to control large segments of a population is to keep them in fear and wanting protection from the police and/or military.

12. Destruction of countries' economies (via Conservative Refocus)

In order to create a new world economy, the Bilderbergers believe that they need to destroy the separate national ones. They plan to achieve this by causing either a long depression that generates decades of decline and poverty, or they plan to use sudden intense economic shocks. These shocks will be similar to the 2006 American housing market collapse. This will allow them to reset national economies into a new alignment with reduced national sovereignty and increased efficiency.

Another example of this process is what is happening in Greece. The economy is in shambles. The country is overloaded with debts that it cannot pay. This now puts the bankers in charge. The bankers now have the intense leverage that they can use to get the government of Greece to go along with the banker's recommended "austerity" programs.

11. *Destruction of the US dollar (via the Balance)*

The Bilderberg Group understands that the destruction of the US dollar is necessary in order to replace it with a world currency. The bankers have been eroding the value of the US dollar for a very long time. A dollar is worth less than 2 percent of what a US dollar was worth one hundred years ago.

US Government officials have been participants in this process, making a mountain of debt that can never be paid back. At some point, it is a mathematical certainty that the US Government's debt will be so huge that it will not be possible to pay the interest on the debt. At that point, the US Government will be forced to default on paying the debt, and America will be bankrupt. The US dollar will become worthless in such a scenario, and that will be the chance to introduce a new global currency.

10. *Population reduction using pandemics (via Ebola YouTube video)*

The enormous growth in the global population and its continued increase is not sustainable over the long term. One way the Bilderberg Group can reduce the human population is by causing pandemics. Biological agents can be intentionally used to cause a major outbreak of illness, which kills millions. Many of the super elite have so little concern for the masses that they consider this the same as culling a herd of animals.

Pandemics may be caused by terrorist groups and also be caused by natural processes. No matter what the cause, as long as the elite can survive the outbreak along with their friends and families, this is all they care about.

9. Media censorship (via the Mancunion)

A Bilderberg member Richard Salant, who was the president of CBS News during the 1960s and the 1970s, explained the Bilderberg Group's influence on media. Salant said, "Our job is not to give people what they want but what we decide they should have."

Media is controlled very heavily by very few companies. Governments actively participate in the censorship of media, as well as promote disinformation if it serves their purpose. The Rockefellers—through their Bilderberg contacts, which include the CEOs of major media companies—gained enormous influence over the media. It is rather hypocritical that these executives from the major news media attend the Bilderberg conferences because they are prohibited from reporting on it.

The censorship goals of the Bilderberg Group are to make views popular by hiding the group's real intent so that these views become public policy. After that, they can pressure governmental leaders and push them in the directions they want them to follow. These are propaganda campaigns that are carefully designed to create public opinion in order to protect corporate power.

8. *Trade zones and trade agreements (via film and digital media)*

The Bilderberg Group starts its process to build its empire by the creation of trade zones and trade agreement that benefits the multinational corporations. They have little interest in any improving the economic levels for the lower classes as long as there are enough of them are able to buy their products.

The jobs all move to the places with the lowest wages, no benefits, and bad working conditions. This allows the multinational corporations to maximize profits. A simple device, like a smartphone that costs around $20 to make, sells at retail for up to $300. It was this type of strategy that made Apple one of the most valuable companies in the world, even though factory workers in Apple's factory in China are jumping out of the windows to commit suicide because of the heavy workload. Apple put up suicide nets outside under the factory windows, yet the working conditions did not change because profits for Apple are soaring.

In the wealthier countries, they keep the consumerism going by issuing credit cards to the consumers. This credit card debt and the high-interest rates one has to pay for it enslaves the average consumer, just like the Bilderberg bankers enslaved the governments.

7. Working for the end of national sovereignty (via nationalunitygovernment.org)

One clear mission of the Bilderberg Group is the end of national sovereignty. In the historical past, the Native American nation was annihilated. The formation of the European Union came about in part by the tremendous influence that the Bilderberg Group members had over their home countries to get them to agree to give up their sovereign rights.

Once member countries join the EU, they no longer have the same level of self-determination. EU regulations are issued, and every member country must follow them. There is no open public debate and no voting on any issue.

Some of the EU regulations can be unfairly balanced, giving more benefits to certain member countries than others. This was the main cause of the Brexit movement, which resulted in the UK leaving the EU. For example, the British fishing industry was decimated by EU regulations, which caused it to lose about 60 percent of the fishing industry in the UK.

6. Creation of the European union (via Euractiv)

Even though the Bilderberg Group's goal is one-world government, they realize this can only be achieved one step at a time. They have already worked on this goal for decades.

25

The steady progress can be seen by studying the historical timeline of the things that led to the formation of the European Union (EU), which are the following:

December 1951—six nations formed the European Coal and Steel Community.

March 1957—six nations signed the Treaty of Rome to form the European Economic Community (EEC) and a second treaty to form the European Atomic Energy Commission (EAEC).

October 1957—the European Court of Justice was formed to handle trade disputes.

May 1960—seven nations formed the European Free Trade Association.

July 1967 saw a merger of the EAEC, the ECSC, with the European Economic Community (EEC).

1968—the European Customs Union was formed to abolish duties and establish uniform import taxes for EEC nations.

1978—the European Currency Unit was created (later changed to the Euro).

February 1992—Maastricht Treaty created the EU on November 1, 1993, and Euros began circulating on January 2002. Euros are now the official currency of sixteen of the twenty EU states.

It took over fifty years for the members of the EU to lose their sovereignty. Up to 80 percent of European laws now are created by nameless, unelected bureaucrats working in or Luxembourg or Brussels. The Bilderbergers are extremely patient in achieving their long-terms goals.

5. *The North American Union (NAU) (via 4.bp. blogspot.com)*

David Rockefeller starting working on the North American Union during the 1980s. He met with Ronald Reagan along with George Schultz and FDA chairman Paul Volker. The first step tried for beginning to create the NAU was to merge Canada with the United States. However, the merger would be without Quebec, where most of the people speak French because Rockefeller thought that was problematic.

They got a Bilderberg-friendly Canadian prime minister elected. The plan would have succeeded except the referendum for Quebec to separate from the rest of Canada was narrowly defeated in 1995. The vote was 50.56% for Quebec to stay as part of Canada and 49.44% for secession.

This defeat did not stop the plans. They started with a trade agreement and, in 1994, created the North American Free Trade Agreement (NAFTA). Then during March 2005 at President George Bush's ranch, a secret meeting was held between Bush, Mexico's president Vincente Fox, and Canada's prime minister Paul Martin. They signed the agreement to form the North American Union (NAU).

Their plan was to surreptitiously create the NAU without involving the legislation of any of the three countries and enforce the merger plan with military force if necessary. They planned to change the currency of the newly borderless North America to the "Amero."

The secret plans were somehow leaked, and once this effort became public knowledge, the plans stopped—at least, for the moment.

4. The Bilderberg Group's intense dislike of Trump (via Fellowship of the Minds)

By taking a look at the names for the June 2016 Bilderberg meeting, it is easy to see that the alignment of the Bilderberg Group was behind Hillary Clinton's run for president of the United States. Senator Lindsey Graham, who is anti-Trump, was at that Bilderberg meeting along with Hillary Clinton.

Donald Trump's campaign included many speeches against globalism and getting rid of what he called bad trade deals like NAFTA. Trump also promised to build a big wall to separate the USA from Mexico, which is exactly the opposite of what the Bilderbergers want. Since Trump did not have to go to the Bilderberg Group for campaign financing or connections, he was able to say such things.

Two weeks after the June 2016 Bilderberg meeting, the Bilderberg Group faced another setback when the UK voted to leave the EU. The Bilderberg Group is in the process of regrouping yet certainly has not been stopped with continuing plans to achieve their goals.

The Bilderberg Group supported the formation of the EU and plans to do more. The plans to form the North American Union that would join Canada, the USA, and

Mexico have changed now when President Trump came into power with the expressed intent to stop such plans. President Trump does not have any idea how strong the Bilderberg Group is, and their plans will continue to develop, albeit slowly. This group is not easy to stop even if some of the founders are dead.

3. Global mind control (via transhumanity.net)

The Bilderberg Group is constantly working with increasing its ability to affect global culture. Other groups know the value of this as well. The Chinese have made significant investments in Hollywood in order to gain enough influence over the content in blockbuster movies. An example of this is the film *The Martian*, where Matt Damian plays an astronaut that is stranded on Mars, and the Chinese help with the rescue.

The Bilderberg Group knows these techniques very well. This is not about censorship, which is excluding content; this method is about having the influence to include content in major blockbuster films that are seen by millions worldwide.

Some of the top Hollywood film directors are of interest to the Bilderberg Group. Jeff Bezos, the founder of Amazon, is also a member. Amazon is building out a digital streaming system for television and films as well as producing their own content. Being able to guide global culture is a form of subtle mind control that can be very effective.

2. Perpetual wars (via Activist Post)

The Bilderberg Group, started by an ex-Nazi, likes to see the continuation of perpetual wars because they are so profitable, and they can fund the needs of both sides. Even if a nuclear war breaks out, there are huge underground cities that are completely self-contained where the elite could live safely.

In the recent air strike on Syria by the USA, twenty-nine Tomahawk missiles were used. Those missiles cost about $1 million each. They are made by Raytheon. To replace them, Raytheon would get a reorder for missiles—a contract worth $29 million. Estimates of the cost of the Mother of All Bombs (MOAB) are around $16 million a piece.

US billion dollars are spent on wars, and the Bilderberg Group members benefit tremendously. The USA has been in so many wars since WWII because it is big business.

1. New World Order—more money and power for the top 0.1% (via humansarefree.com)

Ultimately, the main goal for members of the Bilderberg Group is to keep amazing huge sums of money and gain increasing power to eventually dominate the entire globe. David Rockefeller, who was the last patriarch of the Rockefeller family, died on March 20, 2017. He was the world's oldest billionaire when he died at the age of 101. He died peacefully in his sleep at his home in Pocantico Hills. He certainly did not leave behind a peaceful world—

thanks to the efforts of the Bilderberg Group, the Trilateral Commission, the Council on Foreign Relations, and many other efforts.

Other very powerful Bilderbergers are very old. Henry Kissinger, who was secretary of state under the Richard Nixon administration, is ninety-three years old. George P. Schulz, who was secretary of state under the Ronald Reagan administration, is ninety-six. George Soros is eighty-six years old. Who will fill the power vacuum when all these old school Bilderbergers are gone? That remains to be seen.

The long-term goal for the Bilderberg Group is a borderless world with no nation states, ruled by a one-world government that is controlled by the super elite.

It is not going to be easy to achieve this because the serious wealth inequality, which causes all the money to flow to the top tenth of 1 percent, greatly harms the middle and lower classes. This causes social unrest. Moreover, the massive immigration into Europe—moving from one EU country to another—and the resulting clash of cultures arising from this have destabilized many parts of Europe. The reaction to these negative things that the Bilderbergers want caused a strong rise in nationalism. This is responsible for Brexit to be followed, perhaps by other countries desiring to leave the EU.

Nevertheless, the goal of the Bilderberg Group is one-world government with one global marketplace. The people are to be kept in check by a one-world army and use a single global currency controlled by a one-world bank. The end goal is no less than complete world domination. Every year, the Bilderberg Group's secret meeting advances this agenda steadily toward this goal, even when facing setbacks like the presidency of Donald Trump. (Sources: telegraph.co.uk, independent.co.uk, washingtonpost.com, dailymail.co.uk, express.co.uk)

CHAPTER 26

Here and Now

Whom do you choose? Cultures come and go. God's Word has never changed in over four thousand years, although there is no shortage of attempts to discredit the Word. Bible prophecies have proven dependable, true, and never more so than this very moment in world history.

The prophet Daniel was a righteous man of royal lineage who lived from 620 to 538 BC. Daniel was the second son of King David and Abigail. He was carried off to Babylon as a young man in 605 BC by Nebuchadnezzar, the Assyrian. Daniel was alive when the Medes overthrew Assyria. The Daniel 12 prophecies were sealed until the time of the end—we are there. The reader is challenged to further investigate the prophecies of Daniel.

There is a new uprising against the Jewish people. Let me inform you just who the Jews are. They are human beings whom, centuries ago, God chose to separate from a godless, lawless society to bring law and order into the world, then two thousand years later, a Jewish savior, *Jesus Christ*, to initiate grace for a sinful world. The Law was to educate humanity as to what sin was. Grace through Christ replaced the Jewish law.

Satan has been in a tailspin ever since. He might as well dig a hole and pound sand for all the good he's doing. Satanic influences have caused ethnicities guilty of hating Jews without any legitimate knowledge as to why. Like the idiot Adolph Hitler, a Jew hater, and all those like him, they are part of Satan's army of losers. They strut around, bloviating like proud peacocks. They throw nefarious ideas around like a game of ping-pong and delegate the American people to blind obedience.

Here's a news flash for you: Almighty God's plan can never be defeated or altered. The Jewish people have survived persecution from their inception. They survived slavery in Egypt four hundred years. Hatred for the Jews has raised its ugly head again. Jews and Asians are randomly attacked on our streets, and from what I've seen, the perpetrators were mostly black. This is nothing but orchestrated behavior. Why is this not labeled racism? Can you answer that? Better produce a satisfactory answer because the Bible says that *all* Jews will be saved along with the Christians. "Stick that in your pipe and smoke it."

> The United State is a providential
> nation raised up by divine proclamation.
> America is a major influence in the world
> covering all seven continents. People think
> America's rise to power is coincidence.

> Americas present role in Bible prophesy is no coincidence. Our government is a concept mandated by God, and the authorities that exist instituted by God. God is on the move in America watching over his Word to perform it and fulfill every description that ancient prophecy has spoken concerning America. (Rick Pearson)

Our Founding Fathers deliberately embraced God's ordinances in our constitution. Today, ungodly men are attempting to shred our constitution and champion the burning of our flag. Brutal dictators Hitler, Stalin, Mao, and many others have murdered hundreds of million people throughout history in an attempt to unravel and replace the ordinances of God with secular humanist governments. Millions plus people murdered—really think about that.

God is still here! America has stood in the gap between good and evil along with other nations around the world who want freedom from fascist regimes. Do not be fooled; this is about bringing down America and not about a benevolent government. No, this is a for-profit purpose. This is about America, not a group of people trying to separate the races. Our military protects America from experiencing the devastation of global war on our own soil. Pearl Harbor and the bombing of the World Trade Center are our only exceptions. The powers that be are doing their utmost to dumb down our military. They want us defenseless, so confiscating our guns is a priority.

People were never intended to be manipulated and controlled little robots What is so difficult about distinguishing between love and the evils of hatred? The Lord teaches love and peace. Satan is the origin of evil. This is not rocket science. We only have the two choices. Open your eyes! If you are interested in the origin of good and evil, read the book of Genesis. It's all there and the only logical explanation there is. If you belong to the brainwashed crowd, try Clorox and a little disinfection to your drinking water; it might help. "You only know what you know," and obviously, that's not much.

Hatred itself is a kind of bondage greatly increased by narrow-mindedness, which is ignorance at work. Freedom from this bondage is found through knowledge and understanding, and not through more hate or someone's opinion, including mine. Strive to reach the greatest degree of understanding with the smallest amount of force to gain the good things we desire. Peaceful resistance is not easily attained from disagreeable people steeped in the spread of hatred.

America's enemies hate America and have done their utmost to influence our vulnerable youth from preschool to the towers of higher learning. They promote division, which, of course, is necessary for total control. Pitting child against parent is the left's number one priority. Can hear you now: "I don't believe that." Believe it! The left has about completed the indoctrination. Parents are beginning to speak up, and their voices are heard loud and clear. Enough of critical race theory cluttering our children's brains.

From our inception, we were a nation founded for God's purpose to achieve a government structure that would invoke God's eternal plan. We began school with prayer and the Pledge of Allegiance to our flag, also at sporting events. Once we were called a Christian nation by the men who founded her. Our Founding Fathers were not perfect men. There are no perfect people. We all fall short of the glory of God. This belief definitely drives the leftist autocrats crazy. Obama says on national television, "We are no longer a Christian nation." Could not believe my ears. Only a narcissist would make such a stupid, idiotic statement void of knowledge. Obama does fit that bill. This is the very type of rhetoric gushing from the mouths of our elected government officials. America is on the decline because *they* have denied a holy God. It's past time to wake up, people. Get fanatical!

Those who belong to the Lord will escape the horrors of the tribulation soon facing this world. Would be interesting to see Obama's face when fire consumes his multimillion-dollar mansion on Martha's Vineyard. Just saying!

Ponder this thought: Islam came along about 650 years after Christ, making Islam the new kid on the block striving for dominance. The Islamic holy war has a slightly different purpose than the autocrats seeking world dominance. Islam has hitched its kite to the wrong tail. The pattern is the same from antiquity and will continue until the end of time. Evil men have always sought world dominance through despotic rule over all people and nations. Nothing new under the sun. No matter what evil befalls our nation in the future, all Christians will be delivered from the total devastation facing this present world in the not-so-distant future. Things are moving fast. The devil is on steroids!

> For we do not wrestle against flesh and blood but against principalities, against powers, against the rulers of darkness of this age, against spiritual host of wickedness in the heavenly places. (Ephesians 6:12)

This history of slavery may not be complete, but enough has been recorded and restored to authenticate the facts of this unconscionable practice perpetrated since the dawn of humanity. Despite enraged anger, rioting in our streets, slavery of some kind will never cease to exist somewhere in this present world.

> Only a virtuous people are capable of freedom. As nations become corrupt and vicious, they have more need for masters. (Benjamin Franklin)

> Our Constitution was made only for a moral and religious people. It is wholly inadequate to the government of any other. (John Adams)

All tyranny needs to gain a foothold is
for people of good conscience too remain
silent. (Thomas Jefferson)

Amendment I

Congress shall make no law respecting an establishment of religion or prohibiting the free exercise thereof or
abridging the freedom of speech or of the press or the right
of the people peaceably to assemble and to petition the
government for a redress of grievances.

Amendment II

A well-regulated militia, being necessary to the security of a free state, the right of the people to keep and bear
arms, shall not be infringed.

Our freedoms, plainly stated in the Constitution, are
like no other. We take our freedoms for granted and won't
miss them until they are gone. The American people had
better think long and hard before giving up our freedoms.
Anarchism is placed on the far left of the political spectrum,
and much of its economics and legal philosophy reflect
antiauthoritarian interpretation of left-wing politics, such
as communism, collectivism, syndicalism, mutualism, or
participatory economics. Participatory is a form of socialist
decentralized planned economy, the common ownership

of the means of production, the proposed alternative to capitalism and centralized planning.

If you happen to be one who believes all the disinformation you are fed daily, then why do people leave the failed socialist countries in droves? All who are seeking a better life come to our shores. We never see people breaking into communist countries. Why do we have hundreds of thousands rushing in through our southern borders? I don't believe they are seeking more despotic rule. We have always been known as "the land of the free and the home of the brave." You must come through legal means. Today, undocumented immigrants throughout the world flock to our shores. The American taxpayer foots the hotel bills to house these people—several million to date. They are taken by bus and plane through America in the wee hours of night.

What the Biden administration has done to these desperate people seeking a better life is a travesty of the worse kind. They have no place to go nor a way to earn their keep or even put food in their mouths. Just burden the good old American taxpayer. These children have no future, and many are already sold by unprincipled men peddling sex or drugs. Both Biden and Harris refuse to be seen at the border for fear of the photographs that will live forever. The public is not stupid; we are sick of Kamala running around, talking about root causes. Like Biden, she is reading scripted speeches. Kamala knows nothing about the original root cause of anything. She has become a laughingstock worldwide. Well deserved.

The left plans to eventually eliminate the middle class, then the migrants will fit right into the lower class. They will be Democratic voters, making us a one-party state—no democracy. Migrants will replace many legal industrious American immigrants of all ethnicities. The left famously cloaks its words, so don't fall prey to the rhetoric spewing from the mouths of deceitful politicians. If we do not stand up for America's principles, we fail.

We must also rid our country of the iniquitous sex trade. Foremost, protect our children. Hollywood is number one in producing pornography. I've not spent a dime in theaters for years.

I'm so tired of hearing about systemic racism and woke. Wake up! It's annoying to say the least. This is a Marxist doctrine being pushed upon our children in public schools and universities. The time will come when we will be at war with our children because of the lies they were taught. A Marxist form of racism when embedded through laws within a society or an organization will bring a society to its knees. It can lead to such issues as discrimination in criminal justice, employment, housing, health care, political power, and education, among other issues. This is nothing more than abusive Marxist lies.

Regardless of the situation, lawful or unlawful, it will be justified to the gullible public as a feeble attempt to solve systemic racism. People are running loose like wild animals out of a cage. They bring huge plastic bags into a business, help themselves with no opposition, and apparently no concept of right and wrong. A family member said, "None of that is real. It's all orchestrated for TV." This atrocity must be dealt with soon. Marxists say, "Never let a crisis go to waste." If a crisis is not available, then create one and jump into the middle of the fracas! Nefarious men will always champion chaos among the people. Uninformed, brainwashed masses are foolishly doing the bidding for the fat cats who are resting safely in their multimillion-dollar mansions, reaping the fruits of your labor. Wise up! Don't become goons for the ultrarich.

According to the census, Detroit is 78 percent black and 11 percent non-Hispanic whites. Detroit is now bankrupt. Apparently, the black criminal element refused to change. We can't wait around for someone else to take care of us. Remember, my friend Rat Tail got himself killed in Detroit, or maybe it was Chicago. The south side of Chicago is a war zone. Cities all over America are beset with violence, and this proves what?

People of all races refuse to take responsibility for their failures. Children learn the blame game early in life. People from all races who have become responsible, productive citizens don't sit around wasting time complaining about everything. They worked hard to send their children to school, through college, and set them on the road to a better life. The doors of opportunity have been open for years to all people. Don't blame society for your personal failure to achieve your maximum potential.

The drug culture is no respecter of race, creed, or color. Among other things, adolescents desire social acceptance to impress, to belong, leaving them vulnerable to peer pressure. This opens dark doors of lifelong substance abuse and leaves behind our God-given full potential. Many factors cause substance abuse, including nefarious schemes to destroy our youth, the family, the government, and, finally, America. The political left keep their low-income constituents in tow through welfare, thanks to L. B. Johnson. The American blacks should count their blessings they are not still in darkest Africa or somewhere else in the world. Black people, as all Americans, are free to become anything regardless of welfare's insidious hold on them.

No one profits from listening to Dr. Doom dragging you down, spewing angry rhetoric. Lashing out in anger and resentment will never lead anyone to repentance or responsibility for their own choices. Envy will drive a person to madness. A wise person of any color should ponder on this. Earn respect rather than holding your hands out for reparations. Reparations are nothing more than a Band-Aid, a ruse to satisfy mankind's innate proclivity for greed. You will starve to death depending on government handouts. Learn and secure a trade to sustain you and your family. "If a man will not work, he shall not eat" (1 Thessalonians 3:10). This applies to *all* able-bodied people regardless of creed, color, or race.

Third world Asian immigrants have become successful American citizens Their children are winning spelling bees and getting top SAT scores. Asians are not to blame for the Black people's envious attitudes. Some Black people have allowed envy and hatred to viciously attack Asians just for the thrill of it. Not a thrill, more like a cry for help. Asian parents have taken responsibility for providing a sound education for their children. The need for education is rigidly enforced at home. This is what I say to all you losers: if you don't get it, blame yourself. "Anger abides in the bosom of a fool" (Ecclesiastes 7:9).

Anger is the most dangerous and destructive of all emotions. Anger and depression are all about you—self! God didn't create us this way. "Be angry and do not let the sun go down on your anger, do not give the devil an opportunity" (Ephesians 4:26–27).

Critical race theory is an approach to social philosophy that focuses on assessment and critique of society and culture in order to reveal and challenge power structures. CTR's origins go back to the 1960s and '70s, officially organized in 1989. Critical theory is a social theory directed toward critiquing and changing society as a whole. Critical theories aim to dig beneath the surface of social life and uncover the assumptions that keep human beings from a full and true understanding of how the world works. It's never going to work, pitting one race against another. Envy is pure poison to the soul.

Who died and made these people god? This is nothing more than Marxism. It is also the antithesis of godly teaching. These critical theories expose and challenge the communication of social, economic, and political structures. Political economy focuses on the macro level of communication. As a brainwashing tactic, every word or sentence is prefaced with racist. Before long, we may hear racist car, racist cat, or a racist screwdriver. Enough is enough. Blaming everything on racism has become laughable. Notice all the liberal parrots are in concert on the same days, different channels. Truth, check it out.

Why should we listen to nonsense from a group of intellectuals who, according to historical facts, inevitably get it wrong. Character assassination heads the liberal list and is a direct path to hell; give it up. All you race mongers can bore each other to death after we are gone. I would rather be stuck in traffic or scraping paint than listen to blah, blah, blah. I suggest you take a long hard look at yourselves. Get past the disgusting rhetoric and clean out the political cesspools. This applies to both sides of the aisle.

Critical race theory approaches are Marxism. Again, why should we listen to more nonsense? The goal is division of country, child against parent and family, race against race, etc. This is a horrible injustice to humanity (woke). Just saying. Wrong beyond words. People would rather perish than eat crow. The crow is a carrion eater that is repulsive to eat in the same way that being proven wrong might be emotionally hard to swallow. Too bad. Get over it!

It's asinine to follow an agenda that tears us apart. Rave on, boneheads! Never will I knowingly embrace anything Karl Marx has touched. People breaking into America are leaving communism behind in search of liberty. Unfortunately, in this present climate, the majority will never reach higher than allowed a migrant worker. Of course, all the criminals, dope dealers, and human traffickers will do just fine. Citizens don't leave freedom, and the migrants won't find it here any time soon. The Biden so-called benevolent government is a lie. No, true Americans are not the bad guys. Amen! Thank God parents are beginning to step up to the plate, fighting for our children.

Woke and its definition tells the whole story. Woke is an injustice in society, especially racism. "We need to stay angry and stay woke." It's absurd to fill young minds with hate and envy, especially when repeated time and time again to already weak-minded young individuals regardless of color. In literal terms, woke is being awake and not asleep. The *Oxford Dictionary* expanded its definition of the word *woke* in 2017. Changing our language to fit the narrative of the day is ridiculous. These horrible, inane people want to change woman to "life giver," just to name one of the insane changes. Hear this: I am *awake*, and I rebuke this insipid idea in the name of Jesus Christ.

Marxism is the antithesis of freedom and of Christianity, which is forbidden. There is only one loyalty; the *party* is god. Does the cost of millions of dollars justify the angry, destructive rioting and burning in our cities? Does this demonstrate how the world should work? I think not! If this is an example of how the world should work, then I want no part in this gross injustice to our industrious people of all races, business owners, and schools. Humanity has never been able to *fix* the world's ills, and he never will. Communism certainly cannot because all that Marxism represents is a lie. "Beware of Greeks (Russians) bearing gifts." This timeworn phrase means we should never trust our enemies and should always be on alert. By comparison, God made 7,487 promises to humankind. Some are yet to be fulfilled.

There are no perfect people. God's word says (Old Testament), "An eye for an eye and a tooth for a tooth." Jesus came along and said, "If anyone slaps you on the right cheek, turn to him the other also" (Matthew 5). "Do not avenge yourselves, beloved, but leave room for God's wrath, for it is written, 'Vengeance is mine; I will repay, says the Lord.'" It comforts me to know that God will fight my battles far better than I ever could. I've had no fear of death for most of my life because I know where I came from, why I'm here, and where I'm going. There is nothing here I need or want. Now, that's true peace of heart, mind, and soul. Resting in this comfort zone, and I'm not moving.

Our youth burned flags in the '60s; now flag burning has returned. Will these clueless geniuses ever learn the slightest concept of the freedoms our flag represents? The Philistines might catch on once our freedoms are gone. Youth is oblivious to the future and has limited or no concept of the past, both the good and the evil. Neither do the foggy brains of old leftover druggies who can't see the forest for the trees. Their closed minds live and die in the past. "We only know what we know." Either latch onto the truth or be prepared to face the consequences. Repercussions will eventually reach our shores.

Liberal socialist politicians are out to seize power at all costs, kill our freedoms, change our language, bring down America and all it stands for. We have compared todays chaos with the power-hungry madness of ancient times, each painting the same timeworn subject on a new canvas. The goals remain the same for the wise to ponder. Think! Observing all the negatives that permeated ancient societies should serve as valuable life lessons to remind us of what sin does to a society absent of a holy God. Stand up for righteousness. Remember, no one is perfect, not one! We only act upon what we *think* we know or how we feel. Emotions are unreliable and will lead you through a maze of rabbit trails throughout your entire life if you let them.

Tired of running with the rabbits, Marcia left the maze long ago. Looking back only once finally convinced me. Enough is enough. The Holy Spirit took over, and the rest is history. Learned to put my brain on fire for good use. When I do sometimes jump ahead of God, the faithful Holy Spirit takes the lead. Rather than treating the fire within as my nemesis, God sees it as a power source, perfectly connected to my brain as a fearless contender for the kingdom of God, led by His Holy Spirit. The name Marcia means *warrior*. Ain't that a peach!

We only know what we know. "There are many more things that Jesus did and said. If all of them were written down, not all the books the world could hold them" (John 21:25). Down through the ages, an onslaught of secular men have written volumes upon volumes of every imaginable subject. It is virtually impossible to wade through all the words ever written and come out the other side a sane person standing on a firm foundation. Philosophers are a dime a dozen, peddling their own personal beliefs and convictions concerning life and behavior.

Who died and made these guys God? The Holy Spirit is my one and only confirming source. Just saying! We are bombarded daily with a smorgasbord of opinions coming from all directions. Opinions are just that—opinions. The liberal news channels create the news; they do not report the news accurately. This is a gigantic difference in what is truth or propaganda. Communism is not above lying about anything; they thrive on propaganda.

Personally, I choose the conservative news channels along with the never-changing Bible, brimming with truths that feeds the soul. Today, I'm firmly planted in my reserved place. There isn't a question concerning life that cannot be answered in God's Word, and the Word will never change to appease humankind or placate the current worldview. What a person believes comes from who or what he trusts. Remember, we only know what we know.

Open your minds; compare Big Tech's demands upon our societies with that of God's love and benevolence. One preaches, "Love your fellow man." The other demands total surrender or face censorship. Our children are taught *whiteness* is some kind of incurable disease. It's a good thing *blackness* wasn't taught as an incurable disease. This is all beyond ignorance. There can be no justification for such horrendous, backward teaching by supposedly intelligent human beings. This will one day come back to bit them. This is an insult to the majority of the Black race, other than those drowning in political correctness.

Big Tech will silence every voice that challenges division in their quest for world dominance over all societies. We are restricted from access to posting on our personal Facebook page and Instagram account. Don't dare stick your toe in democratic forbidden waters lest a band of piranhas devour your entire leg in seconds. When the American people get sick and tired of being sick and tired of their chains being yanked, the herd will come alive. Then look out—trouble! *Red Handed* by Peter Schweizer is a wonderful informative read. It may soon be banned—the truth is poison to liars.

Biden's latest remarks on live TV blew me away. The subject was gun control, the Second Amendment, the right to bear arms, and confiscating our guns. "What you do doesn't matter. We can just nuke you." I heard this with my own ears. Amen. No doubt this man is finally off his rocker. Biden was probably punished for that remark; think *they* made him stand in a corner?

This is frightening. People are committing crimes all the time, not ever held accountable. Prosecutors paid by George Sorus do nothing to uphold the law. What law? The same with judges, no bail, defund the police, thus the explosion of the welfare state. There is nothing positive coming out of our government. Why would any sane person choose to give up freedom to live under the iron fist of a central control? As you should have learned from ancient history, blind obedience is demanded and brutally enforced.

> Freedom is a fragile thing and it's never more than a generation away from extinction. We didn't pass it to our children in the bloodstream. It must be fought for. (Ronald Reagan)

There is nothing new under the sun. World history covers so much more than I have related. I do not claim to be an expert on the subject of world history. I do understand what took place from WWI forward to WWII because I was from that generation. I have relied on the works of others to guide me through these pages, enabling me to tell this story. The knowledge gained through these studies has broadened the scope of my understanding beyond any expectations. Hopefully, you will say the same. Bravo if you have gotten this far.

One last plug for creation. We didn't evolve from yuck. Canadian geese migrations can be as long as two thousand to three thousand miles. If the weather is right, they can fly as much as 1,500 miles a day. This requires order and discipline. The geese fly in a perfect V formation, flapping their wings, creating an uplifting air. When the lead goose tires, he drops back, and another takes his place. This is God's perfection at work.

Rainbow trout spawn in late spring; brown trout spawn in the fall. Both species return to the same streams and rivers where they were born to spawn. Salmon also return to the stream they were born from to spawn and to die. Atlantic salmon do not die after spawning, so adults can repeat the spawning cycle for several years. Scientists believe that salmon navigate by using the earth's magnetic field like a compass. When they find the river they came from, they start using smell to find their way back to their home streams—another example of God's timeless perfection at work.

Nature has no choice. It does what it was created to do and right on time. In that sense, nature is orderly; there is a time and season for everything. Yet in nature's fallen state, it doesn't all perfectly fulfill its purpose. Animals live by instinct. Humankind is not so orderly because man was given choices. Because we were allowed to make choices, we inevitably choose to lean upon our own understanding.

Both man and nature will remain in a fallen state until Jesus sets up His kingdom on earth, where there will be no death and no disease. "We know that all creation has been groaning as in the pains of childbirth right up to the present time" (Romans 8:22). I rest my case! "The lamb will lie down with the lion" (Isaiah 65:25, 11:6–7). This will happen when Jesus rules over His government on earth, a time when all of creation will be at peace.

Remember, you only know what you now. If nothing I have said registers with you now, when these things happen, and they will, your brain will perk up. Those of you who refuse to listen to anyone or anything foreign to your fixed mindset will have the opportunity to flex your angry muscles again. Remember, irrelevance is stupid! My hope is that you will take a new path, making a concerted effort to search out these truths in more detail. Try waking up your innate powers of reasoning that have been in a coma for the greater part of your life. God hasn't slighted anyone. Always weigh the cost. These truths are learned and activated through knowledge.

For the Christian, faith comes through knowledge of God's Word. Faith activates the power of the Holy Spirit within us. Think about it. You will be rewarded for your effort. We must all stand up for truth and hold our politicians responsible, or we may wake up in a bed crawling with worm slime. Nothing can replace the freedom and peace of mind enlightened through the godly principles our nation was founded on. God has surely blessed America.

Do not lean on your own understanding. There is nothing new under the sun. You only know what you know. So ask and keep on asking, seek and keep on seeking, and knock and keep on knocking (Matthew 7:7–8, Luke 11:9–10). The Creator of the universe will answer with His open door (John 10:7, 9; Acts 16:26).

PS: While editing this book, Putin invaded Ukraine. This would have never happened on President Trump's watch. Joe Biden, on day one, took away our energy independence and then bought oil from Russia, thereby financing Putin's war! Perhaps Putin has blackmail information on Biden and his family, or he just disrespects the man. Now Biden is begging Saudi Arabia to increase oil production to lower the price of oil and gas. They refused. See how history is painfully repeating itself à la Neville Chamberlain's weak position inviting Hitler to trample Europe. Nothing new under the sun. You only know what you know. C'est la vie!

ACKNOWLEDGMENTS

My love and gratitude to my daughter Karen and husband Courtney Coe for their never-ending incredible generosity. I just casually mentioned I might like to write a book. The next thing I know, I'm the proud owner of a twenty-eight-inch screen, computer, and a new laser printer—truly a gift of unconditional love. Without a computer, this book would have never been possible. Your love and loyalty precede you. "God loves a cheerful giver" (2 Corinthians 9:7). Bless you and thank you.

I am grateful to Marion Gebhardt, who edited my manuscript in its infancy, getting me off to a roaring start. Marion is a friend, and he is also my bridge partner in competitive tournaments. Marion is a very fine player and also a Christian.

I am grateful to all who prayed for success on my journey as a new author. Thanks to each of you. I would be remiss not to praise the wonderful Holy Spirit, who lives in my head and heart, guiding my thoughts and guiding my fingers across the keyboard.

I could search the world over and may never find another neighbor like Diane Blythe. She is not only a precious Christian but my computer counselor, and she never fails to answer my call for help. She also never failed to quickly solve the problems I created—I'm computer challenged. Diane writes scriptures in beautiful calligraphy on broken pieces of marble. They are outstanding and sold throughout the world. Thank you, my sweet generous lady, for who you are in Christ and for being my friend. There would be no book without your faithful generosity at my beck and call.

Thanks to all who labored before me for the incredible references available on any subject, without which I am at a loss for words.

REFERENCES

Dr. Shashi Tharoor, *World History*.
www.bbc.co.uk
www.Britannica.com
www.facinghistory.org
www.wsj.com/blccb
www.newslearningonline.com
www.govinfo.gov
www.smithsonianmag.com
www.independent.com.uk
www.bbc.com/news
www.history.com
www.newslineinstitute.org
www.BibleGateway.com
www.wikipedia.com
www.bilderbergmembers.wordpress.com/bilderberg-mem-bers-current/
www.theclever.com/20-shocking-facts-about-the-bilder-berg-group/

ABOUT THE AUTHOR

Marcia developed her oil painting skills early in life and now paints an intimate portrait of her first eight years of life in French Settlement, Louisiana, a Cajun French community along a South Louisiana Bayou, where her father was the school principal. As both parents were Christians, Marcia embraced a love for the Lord early in life. She spent wonderful summers with cousins on the Hutchison cotton farm in North Mississippi.

Marcia has learned the importance of faith, family, and the unique joys and trials of life. She is the mother of six children, who produced thirty offspring.

Marcia has enjoyed extensive world travels, then has captured her memories on canvas. She is a master bridge player, saying the competition keeps the old brain alive. Many other life-changing experiences occurred along the way, some for the good and some not so good. Marcia understands that all her clumsy yesterdays are the substance of her existence, all in much need of redemption. Turning back to the Lord was like the first day of her life, the onset of new beginnings.